PRAISE FOR *REAL SEX*

'Real Sex *is a revelation, a prescription and a relief! Finally –
a book about pleasure, not performance, that helps us reclaim
our innate erotic intelligence, an intelligence that has been
subverted by both the media and the porn industry.* Real Sex
gets a high five and a huge thank you from me. Read it.'
DR CHRISTIANE NORTHRUP, *NEW YORK TIMES* BESTSELLING AUTHOR OF
GODDESSES NEVER AGE AND *WOMEN'S BODIES, WOMEN'S WISDOM*

'Mike and Louise have prompted me to look at sex in a whole new
way that I'd genuinely class as revolutionary and profound. Their
work goes way beyond what happens between the sheets. Its impact
resonates positively through so many areas of my life; it's as though
they bashed the 'Gong of Wrong' in my head, and the reverberations
have been echoing through my psyche ever since, highlighting the
previously broken ways I was viewing myself, my relationships and
my intimate interactions, and evolving them into more constructive,
illuminated ways of thinking. This is a book that won't only improve
what happens in your bed, but also what happens in your head.'
ALIX FOX, SEX EDUCATOR, JOURNALIST AND BROADCASTER

'As a model I've spent the past 10 years working with my body,
but thanks to Louise and Mike I'm learning how to unlearn all the
distorted messages society has bestowed on me and I'm trying to strip
down to my true core to access what my desire looks, sounds and
feels like. We live in such a shame-driven world, and as a millennial
I see the positive impact of the Internet but also the negative effects
of social media, which can make us feel more isolated and insecure
than ever. Mike and Louise's relationship, as well as their work
as therapists, is a true inspiration. I urge everyone to pick up this
absolutely essential book and start accessing your sexuality so that
we can connect to ourselves and others on a real level, and be free!'
NAOMI SHIMADA, MODEL/DOCUMENTARY FILMMAKER

REAL SEX

REAL SEX

Why Everything You Learned
About Sex Is Wrong

MIKE LOUSADA AND LOUISE MAZANTI PhD

HAY HOUSE

Carlsbad, California • New York City • London
Sydney •Johannesburg • Vancouver • New Delhi

First published and distributed in the United Kingdom by:
Hay House UK Ltd, Astley House, 33 Notting Hill Gate, London W11 3JQ
Tel: +44 (0)20 3675 2450; Fax: +44 (0)20 3675 2451
www.hayhouse.co.uk

Published and distributed in the United States of America by:
Hay House Inc., PO Box 5100, Carlsbad, CA 92018-5100
Tel: (1) 760 431 7695 or (800) 654 5126
Fax: (1) 760 431 6948 or (800) 650 5115
www.hayhouse.com

Published and distributed in Australia by:
Hay House Australia Ltd, 18/36 Ralph St, Alexandria NSW 2015
Tel: (61) 2 9669 4299; Fax: (61) 2 9669 4144
www.hayhouse.com.au

Published and distributed in the Republic of South Africa by:
Hay House SA (Pty) Ltd, PO Box 990, Witkoppen 2068
info@hayhouse.co.za; www.hayhouse.co.za

Published and distributed in India by:
Hay House Publishers India, Muskaan Complex, Plot No.3, B-2,
Vasant Kunj, New Delhi 110 070
Tel: (91) 11 4176 1620; Fax: (91) 11 4176 1630
www.hayhouse.co.in

Distributed in Canada by:
Raincoast Books, 2440 Viking Way, Richmond, B.C. V6V 1N2
Tel: (1) 604 448 7100; Fax: (1) 604 270 7161; www.raincoast.com

A catalogue record for this book is available from the British Library.

ISBN: 978-1-78180-824-5

Interior images: Liron Gilenberg | www.ironicitalics.com

CONTENTS

ACKNOWLEDGEMENTS

This book is dedicated to all the longing hearts that are waking up to the journey of real, embodied, loving connection with themselves and others.

We are immensely grateful to Jovanna Desmarais, Sophia Swire and Claudia Shaffer, who sent us in the right direction; to Rex Brangwyn, David and Simon Confino, who shared their ideas; and to Amy Kiberd and Michelle Pilley at Hay House for receiving us with enthusiasm. Thank you to the Boys and to Lottie for keeping our hearts open, despite the physical distance.

Introduction

WHY EVERYTHING YOU LEARNED ABOUT SEX IS WRONG

There is something missing from our culture, something fundamental to our happiness as human beings. Without it, our lives will never be fulfilled. We'll never feel the sense of balance and harmony that we long for. That something is a healthy relationship with our sexuality – for while society pushes sex in our faces every day, we still find ourselves disconnected from it.

This book will explain why a healthy relationship with our sexuality is so important for leading a meaningful life. It offers a new, integrated idea of sexuality that allows for modern technological developments and for pornography (which is here to stay, whether we like it or not), and holds a positive outlook on our future as the sexual beings that we are.

Over its seven main chapters, the book sets out seven essential ways – Seven Keys – for us to learn to be real with ourselves and with our partners. It's these Seven Keys that can lead to 'real sex' – deep, fulfilling and meaningful intimacy, both physical and emotional; intimacy where we can show up authentically, with all our needs, insecurities, our true power and our desires, instead of leaning on the distorted messages we've received from society. We'll show you that by having 'real sex' you'll not only improve your sex life, but also expand your experience of yourself and your ability to have better, deeper relationships.

We, the authors, live and practice what we teach. There is little difference for us between life and work. In the years of developing professional skills in this field, our own journey into intimacy has transformed who we are and how we relate to one another as we've uncovered and integrated our own insecurities, shame and challenges. As sex therapists (or 'Love Revolutionaries', as we like to call ourselves), we've developed the Seven Keys over many years of professional and personal experience.

In writing this book, we have called on our experience to help you, like the thousands of men, women and couples we have seen in our private practices, to reclaim your sexuality, expand your pleasure and deepen the intimacy with yourself and with your partners or lovers. We've dedicated our lives to healing the collective wounds of sex and intimacy because we believe that each person's ability to love to the fullest, and to manifest what we're all deeply longing for, depends on our ability to connect with life itself – the life that is running through our bodies when we are free to fully express our sexuality.

In our approach we look beyond sex as a physiological function and at the importance of intimacy and body-mind connection when it comes to the sexual experience.

This book also shows that, ultimately, sexuality can act as a gateway to connecting with those forces that are greater than ourselves, forces that some may label as 'divine'. It explains that 'real sex' is a deeper, more connected way of engaging with our sexual and life-force energies that allows us to expand our sense of who we are, and how we relate to others, with honesty and integrity.

SEXUALITY AS A PILLAR OF LIFE

Imagine life as a classical Greek temple. At the base there's the foundation, rising from which are several pillars. At the top is the triangular pediment section. Imagine that the foundation is our culture, our community, the collective society in which we live. The pediment represents what we all aspire to: aliveness, passion, love, connection, meaning, purpose.

Now visualize the pillars that support this pediment. Each pillar stands for a different path to our aspiration. We might follow the path of the mind – learning, teaching, thinking, articulating, exploring philosophies or conducting scientific research into the mysteries of life, and so on. This is a valid path towards a meaningful life. Another pillar is embodiment – finding meaning through action: through sport or physical activities. We feel our aliveness when engaging our bodies, testing them, expanding their capacity through challenge and competition (with either ourselves or others), seeking the perfection of physical endeavour.

Yet another pillar is devotion – the spiritual path of meditation, prayer, religion, awareness and so on. Spiritual practices can help us to feel a deep sense of purpose in our lives, to stretch towards the sense of wholeness that we're longing for and to take our consciousness to deeper levels of being. Feeling and emotion form another pillar, one that requires us to empathize, sense, feel for others, care for them, to give and receive, perform healing, charity, sustainability or care work, or build up a family or a community – all giving us a sense of meaning and purpose.

A further pillar is aesthetics and creativity. Self-expression through the arts, movement, dance and creativity in all its forms can help us to feel that aliveness, that sense of joy and meaning. Art can connect us to something greater than ourselves – a force beyond the mundane that expresses the depth of the human soul and the height of aesthetic perfection.

Each one of these pillars is essential to our wellbeing, to our relationship with life itself. Each one supports and nourishes our connection to a deeper experience of being alive. However, there's one pillar that's missing. It is cast down, lying broken upon the earth. This is the pillar of sexuality. It has been misappropriated by commercialism, by fear, by shame – and it lies toppled, present in our culture but no longer supporting the temple of our aliveness. Without the pillar of sexuality the temple does not stand complete. Without it, our aspirational pediment is askew, at risk of tumbling down.

The purpose of this book is to begin to return the pillar of sexuality to its rightful place alongside the others. In fact, sexuality is arguably the most important of the pillars because it requires us to engage all the aspects represented by the other pillars:

> *To have truly great, fulfilling sex we must engage the mind, the body, our feelings and our creativity.*

EROTIC INTELLIGENCE

Most people have heard of emotional intelligence – that is, the skill of interacting with others and the ability to recognize and name different emotional states in both ourselves and other people. Emotional intelligence is, of course, fundamental to a deep and healthy relationship, be it friendship or romantic connections. However, as pre-eminent developmental psychologist Howard Gardner argues with his 'multiple intelligences' theory,[1] there are also other types of intelligence. Among them, Gardner cites what he calls 'bodily-kinesthetic' intelligence – the ability to sense where our body is in physical space in relation to itself and other things or people, and the ability to control our movements, posture and timing; for example, the ability to know that your hand is resting on your knee or is moving upwards. Another that Gardner lists is linguistic intelligence – an aptitude for words and the ability to communicate clearly and meaningfully to describe our experience.

> *Like the pillars of our temple, there's a place for each of the different ways we can be intelligent.*

However, it could be argued that there's one form of intelligence, not specified by Gardner, that's more complex, richer and more essential than any other – and that is erotic intelligence. Erotic intelligence requires us to develop skills in all the other forms of intelligence in order for it to be fully established. A full and healthy relationship with our sexuality requires us to have intelligence that is emotional, intrapersonal (having self-awareness of our own internal thoughts, processes, hopes and fears), interpersonal (understanding the dynamics of relationships between ourselves and others), bodily, linguistic and creative. In fact, sexuality requires us to develop a broader range of intelligence than any other part of human experience, with the possible exception of child rearing. This makes sexuality one of the key pillars of the human experience and personal growth.

With the Seven Keys to 'real sex' that we have defined in this book, we will help you develop your erotic intelligence, and reclaim your healthy, free and natural sexuality. The problem is that in our culture sexuality has been hijacked. Powerful groups have distorted our relationship with sexuality so that we've become confused, disoriented and judgmental about it.

The forces of commercialism have made sexuality a commodity, something to be bought and sold.

The medical profession has been making major inroads on our sexuality, telling us what dysfunctions and pathologies we have, with these leading to so-called cures, whether pharmacological, medical or cosmetic. Best known of these is Viagra, annual sales of which peaked in 2008 at just under $2 billion, and in 2016 the US Food and Drug Administration has approved flibanserin (sold as Addyi), dubbed the 'female Viagra'. This potentially opens the gateway for a large number of pharmacological solutions to female desire issues, issues that are far more likely to arise from the cognitive and emotional issues addressed in this book. Meanwhile, governments seek to control what we do sexually by banning or allowing certain sexual acts, such as homosexuality, or by the subtle control of what information is given to citizens such as pre-teenagers, the disabled, gender-fluid and the elderly.

WHAT OUR SOCIETY SUPPRESSES

In our culture, there are two primal forces that we don't deal with very well. One is anger. In a 'civilized' society we're persuaded that anger is not a healthy emotion, so much of it is suppressed and what is permitted to be expressed is directed towards those we stigmatize and vilify, such as paedophiles or so-called Islamic State. These groups are seen as the dangerous 'other' upon which we're allowed to vent our rage because they are perceived as monstrous evils.

The other force that our culture doesn't deal with well is desire.

We are encouraged to want things, not experiences.

Our commercially orientated society tells us the healthy place to direct our desire is at this gadget or that handbag, not towards physical pleasure and certainly not towards sex, unless it's within the socially acceptable conditions that our culture tolerates; in other words, within a monogamous relationship.

However, this limiting and distorted perspective is part of what has caused the pillar of our sexuality to tumble from the temple of life. No matter what new gadget we buy, what fabulous new dress we acquire or what new relationship we find ourselves in, our deepest longing won't be fully met unless we include our sexuality in that temple.

For so many people, sex has become about performance – that is, they become more concerned with what it looks like, and about how they appear to others, than their own experience. Consider the case of our client Jenny, when she comes to us for help with what she thinks are her sexual issues. She is absolutely gorgeous: rich, golden hair cascades in loose curls to her shoulders, framing a stunningly attractive face with fine features, perfectly made up. Her figure-hugging black summer dress is just sheer enough to hint at lacy panties, and she's not wearing a bra. But she looks anguished. 'Please,' she says. 'You've got to help me. I feel terrible. It's really affecting my life. I need to learn how to give the best handjob ever.'

Sounds like soft porn? In reality, this is a situation that occurs quite regularly in our therapy rooms. Many men and women, often successful and well-adjusted in so many other areas of their life, come in asking if we can teach them sexual techniques to make them better lovers. So why is it that so many generally confident people feel inadequate and insecure in the bedroom? Why is it that so many people you'd imagine to have no problem attracting sexual or romantic partners struggle so much to find them or keep them?

This book explains why pretty much everything our society has tried to teach us about our sexuality is misplaced, misleading or simply wrong. It explores how our society has created so many distortions around sex that many of the things we thought made for great sex are barriers rather than benefits. We'll look at how the media, particularly pornography, has created a culture around sexuality that sets unrealistic expectations and offers false promises. The media has told us that sex is about orgasm and that it's about how we look or what we do during sexual interactions. When not making sex itself morally questionable, most modern sex myths focus on performance – how to have or give the best orgasm, different positions, sexual 'tricks' such as female ejaculation or fashionable kink scenarios.

This is not only misguided, but it also actually creates a society that has more, not fewer, hang-ups about sex; hang-ups based on ideas that are, in fact, ill-informed and are contributing to a more sexually dysfunctional society rather than a move towards a sexual utopia.

Today's sexual culture is destined for deeper anxiety
and greater disconnection from our sexuality,
our partners and, ultimately, ourselves.

REAL SEX

In this book we offer an alternative to the unattainable ideas and images of perfection peddled by the media. The book is not intended to provide therapy for those with traumatic sexual histories or sexual dysfunction, though it can support them. Nor is it a 'how-to' guide to 365 techniques for sexual ecstasy or a tantric text encouraging sex as the path to spiritual enlightenment, though it offers an element of this. Instead, it brings new perspectives on what sex – 'real sex' – is and what it means.

We're aiming to help you to understand how to experience 'real sex' – living, breathing, fulfilling sex that's an authentic expression of who you are, not an attempt to copy mental images of who you think you ought to be.

We'll approach this by helping you to unlearn the confusing messages you've probably picked up about sex and by revealing the deeper experience of sex. We'll explain how variety can arise not only from doing new things in sex, but also – and more significantly – from allowing different parts of yourself to be expressed sexually.

We'll look at how pornography and media culture in general have created a distorted view of sexuality, and explain why this hinders so many people in having 'real sex', in some cases creating a new wave of psychological and sexual issues for both men and women. Our method offers an antidote to the impulse for instant penetration, using an approach that leads not only to better, but also to longer-lasting and more pleasurable sex.

Throughout the book you'll be guided on a journey into your sexuality through a series of exercises to practise at home. These exercises will open you to your own personal, authentic expression of your sexuality in its fullness. You'll be helped to overcome the blocks you have towards intimacy and will learn new tools to help you enjoy your sexuality in a new way. Whether you're in a relationship of many years' standing or are single and struggling to find love and sexual satisfaction, this book will offer you guidance on transforming your relationship with sexuality, and ultimately with yourself, in ways that might surprise you.

We also follow the stories of men and women who, like Jenny (cited earlier), have come to us to work on issues around their sexuality and who have had problems with intimacy. Perhaps you will see something of yourself in their stories. We hope they demonstrate how people with challenging problems with sex have been able to overcome them using our method.

As described, the method sets out the seven principles – our Seven Keys – that lead to what we call 'real sex' – deep, fulfilling and meaningful intimacy, both physical and emotional. By following the Seven Keys, you will undertake a journey to the heart of your sexual self, a journey that will reveal hidden meanings of sexuality to you, and will help you to overcome your blocks and resistances to having authentic, pleasurable, 'real sex'. Clients like Jenny may come to us originally because they wish to learn new positions or techniques, but they soon realize this is not where the problem lies. Their blocks to intimacy lie not in what they do, but in how they feel. The Seven Keys will allow you to change your relationship with your sexuality in a way that will let you enjoy it more fully.

Ultimately, this is a journey of transformation that will help you to integrate your sexuality more healthily and freely into your sense of who you are.

WHAT'S WRONG WITH SEX IN OUR SOCIETY TODAY?

In our society, there's no area in which healthy integration is needed more than in our sexuality. On the one hand, sexuality is now ubiquitous; it is more accessible and more acceptably discussed than at perhaps any other time in recent history. On the other hand, media and porn imagery create a distorted expectation of sexuality.

This imagery can easily give the impression of a society where everyone except you is able to experience different types of wonderful climactic sex on a more or less constant and readily achievable basis. It also heaps pressure on us to look or act a particular way.

> *While we may recognize that this is media hype and that the images shown in pornography are not reality, the insidious nature of pornographic and soft-porn images used by the media enables them to infiltrate our unconscious.*

They then raise our bar of expectation, both of ourselves and our partners, to unrealistic levels. We'll explore this in more detail in the next chapter.

Part of the problem of the omnipresence of sexual imagery, be it in pornography or in the media, is that sex is almost constantly in our awareness. That doesn't mean we're always thinking about sex, but that we're repeatedly exposed to the subtle, invasive messages about sexuality that our culture throws at us. This act of bringing sexuality into our awareness is both a gift and a burden. The benefit is that sexuality becomes more accessible and more acceptable; people are, in general, more open about their sexuality than they used to be and there's greater acceptance of individuals' sexual freedom and self-expression. The burden, however, is that by having our culture's sexual norms in our heads so actively, we're frequently running internal dialogues about what sex is meant to look or feel like. This prescriptive view of sex limits our ability to enjoy our own experiences or to have unconventional desires.

Both society and pornography depict a very specific form of sexual identity that tells us there's a right amount of sex that we should be having. It also tells us that there's a right kind of sex and sexual desire. If we don't desire sex, we become 'wrong' and psychology and medical professionals will quickly tell us we're suffering from some type of sexual dysfunction. In recent years, new psychological 'disorders' have been named to pathologize those who don't exhibit the socially acceptable amount of sex drive. Labels such as Female Sexual Arousal Disorder, Sexual Aversion Disorder, Female Orgasmic Disorder and Hypoactive Sexual Desire Disorder are just a few of the many clinical diagnoses that patients may receive if suffering from a lack of sexual desire.

Similarly, if we want too much sex we may also be pathologized, particularly in the case of women. There was a strong argument for including hypersexual disorders (having too much desire) in the fifth edition of the US 'bible' of psychiatric disorders, the *Diagnostic and Statistical Manual of Mental Disorders*. This argument was only narrowly defeated yet pressure remains to stigmatize those who desire sex 'too much' as sex 'addicts', and the topic of sex addiction is increasingly in people's awareness. So, society tells us that we should want sex enough, but not too much. Anything outside this narrow and restrictive range is considered abnormal and unhealthy.

Society and pornography place on us an enormous burden of expectation. We easily fall into unfavourable comparison with the idealized imagery we're subjected to daily.

> *We tend to judge both ourselves and others*
> *against an unrealistic set of standards*
> *that can never be met and can lead only to*
> *dissatisfaction and emotional distress.*

Pornography, with its typically limited depiction of what is perceived as sexually attractive, is a significant part of this process. We focus not on the positives of our sexual experience but on the inadequacies. This creates an internal dialogue that tells us we're not good enough in one way or another, depending on our view of sexuality.

By believing this internal dialogue, we lose our connection with ourselves and consequently with the other person, too. If we're lost in internal imagery while having sex or connecting intimately with others, we can't fully feel our experience of being present in our body and enjoying sex. If we're not present in our own experience – in our bodily sensations, our emotions and our pleasure – during sexual interactions, we won't be able to be present with our partner. This disconnection leads to a lot of sexual dissatisfaction and forms the basis of many relationship failures.

WHY DOES SEX MATTER?

We've already looked at how erotic intelligence is perhaps the most sophisticated form of intelligence we can acquire because it depends on us accessing so many other forms of our intelligence. When we engage with these multiple forms of intelligence we must also engage with what we do not have or what we fear will happen. It's through our sexuality, therefore, that we're faced with our deepest longings and our deepest fears and vulnerabilities. Developing our sexual self is core to our sense of identity and for our relationship with life itself. Most of us want to improve our sexual lives, but addressing our relationship with sex is much more far-reaching than just having better and more intimate sex.

When we really look into our relationship with our sexuality, we're altering not only our whole sense of who we are as a person but also our brain chemistry. This is key to profound change. Neuroscientists now recognize that the brain is 'plastic', meaning that it can develop new neural pathways that lead to new behaviours, new experiences of ourselves and a healthier, more positive sense of who we are. The brain is not a fixed, hard-wired organ but one that is constantly changing and developing. This is good news because if we feel negative about ourselves, for example sexually, there's the potential for change.

In order to develop new behaviours, new ways of thinking and new emotional experiences we need to develop new neural pathways. One of the fastest ways to create new neural pathways that lead to positive changes is by having experiences that combine moderate levels of stimulation or arousal and a meeting between one person and another.

Louis Cozolino, psychology professor at Pepperdine University, California also lists new physical and emotional experiences among his essential criteria for positive neural growth[2] – changing the way the cells in our brain form neural pathways to create positive mental shifts. Each one of Cozolino's key criteria allows the brain to grow stronger cellular connections that create a new understanding of who we are, how we feel about ourselves and how we interact with the world. Interestingly, each of Cozolino's criteria is also present in a positive sexual experience.

> *Sex is not just about sex. It's also about our emotional development and growth, both personal and between yourself and others.*

In fact, sex seems to be the most powerful tool we have for personal growth. It's in the cauldron of sexuality that all of our fears and vulnerabilities arise. It's in sex that we're invited to step beyond our comfort zones. Beyond them we perceive an alarming 'otherness', an energy or quality with which we are unfamiliar and which may well terrify us. Sex is the ultimate tool for personal empowerment and fulfilment – not in a hedonistic way, but in a more profound sense, of feeling full within oneself. Sex is the place where mind, body and emotions all meet. And sex is the most effective instrument we know for the integration and deepening of relationships. The more authentically we can have sex, the more authentic we can be in the world. No wonder sex is so emotionally charged and challenging for so many of us.

WHAT CAN THIS BOOK DO FOR YOU?

This book isn't simply a guide to having 'real sex'. It also explains how to step more fully into your sexuality and how to use this as a portal into how you feel about yourself, acting as a booster for your personal growth. Ultimately, it aims to take you on a journey into the heart of your sexual self.

We explain our Seven Keys, designed to bring you greater awareness of yourself. They will help you to understand the nature of your desires, what you actually long for sexually and how you can obtain this. You'll become more at peace with your sexual desires and learn the deeper motivations behind your sexual longings and turn-ons. The book will also teach you communication skills and help you to develop stronger personal boundaries – something that's essential for having 'real sex'.

By following the exercises in this book, you will learn to love and accept your mind, body, feelings and sexuality at a deeper level. You'll be able to change your relationship with your body and learn that every part of you can provide a source of pleasure.

As you travel inwards at the start of your journey, you will renegotiate your relationship with your own sexuality. Doing so will help you to integrate it more fully and more harmoniously into your sense of who you are. This creates new neural pathways in your brain that help you to establish clear, positive messages about sexuality in your subconscious. These, in turn, impact the unconscious messages that you send out into the world.

> *However much you long for a different type of relationship or sexual experience in your life, you are unlikely to find it without changing your internal dialogues about your own sexuality.*

Once these internal changes have begun, you can start to look at your relationship with the outside world.

AN AGENT OF CHANGE

Have you ever noticed the kind of person who walks into a room and seems to grab everyone's attention instantly? Have you ever seen people who seem full of sexuality, no matter what they are doing? These people know the secret. They've made internal shifts within themselves about how they feel about their own sexuality and through doing so send out a different type of message into the world – and the world responds to those messages.

In this book we'll share with you the secrets to creating those changes. When you've made them, people will respond naturally and effortlessly to you and you'll be able to attract the type of man or woman you are longing for and who previously felt unattainable.

> *If you are already in relationship, you'll become*
> *the force of change that helps your partner change*
> *their behaviour to meet your needs more fully.*

You may also notice that your friends start telling you that you're looking younger or more vibrant. Perhaps you'll get more attention from men or women. Perhaps your partner will start relating to you in a new and different way. You're likely to change not only how you have sex but how you feel about the type of sex you are having. The messages you send out into the world will alter how you make yourself available, and who and what types of connection with others you attract will transform your experience of yourself and your sexuality.

The more you integrate different parts of your sexual self into who you are, the more parts of yourself you will access and the fuller you'll become as a person. You'll become more empowered, more able to make choices, to have influence and be effective in the world. This allows you to exist in the world more authentically and to express yourself more fully; you'll no longer need to hide or suppress parts of yourself.

Transforming your relationship with your sexuality will then have the power to change things not only internally, but also externally. By feeling more confident you are likely to find new ways to express yourself, not just sexually but also creatively; sex is a powerful creative force. Of course, sex can have the potential to create new life, but it's linked to creative expression, too. At our practice, we've found that working with people's sexuality leads directly to greater creative expression.

> *People who are more in touch with their sexuality*
> *start to paint, to draw, to sing, to learn that*
> *musical instrument they always wanted to.*

Many artists or creative people who have come to us with sexual issues have often suffered from creative blockages, but these have melted away once they've integrated their sexuality more deeply into themselves.

This book can also help you to remove the taboos and myths our society holds around sex; there are so many that it's sometimes hard to know what is sexually acceptable and what is not. Instead of taboo, we invite you to consider that your sexuality is your natural, creative life-force energy.

TOWARDS SEXUAL EMPOWERMENT

Let's not forget that we come from a very long line of sexually motivated organisms. For 4 billion years, each of your ancestors successfully managed to have sex and reproduce. If any of them had failed, you wouldn't be reading this book. Four billion years makes for a lot of neural programming and a lot of evolutionary imperative. Sex, then, is your lifeblood, and irrespective of your gender it's your evolutionary impulse and your essential life-force energy.

The question is, how much of this life-force energy do you truly allow yourself to express? How much sexual energy can you hold and how much do you deny yourself? How much do you edit out your desires and your sexual needs?

> *If you edit out much of your sexual self, how*
> *can you hope to truly feel who you are?*

Can you be fully alive and experience life in all its rich fullness if you can't feel your sexual life-force energy? It's unlikely. This book will help you to access your sexual aliveness more fully, to express it healthily and in an integrated way. This way, it will help you to gain a deeper knowledge of your whole self.

Be warned, however: to access this part of yourself is dangerous. You may unsettle existing relationship dynamics. You may discover a new sense of empowerment. You may start to ask for what you want and cease to put up with sex or relationships that don't meet your needs. In short, the established order may be destabilized and new paradigms of empowerment may emerge.

The power dynamic that so often exerts itself in sex is interesting and it can be fascinating to see who in our culture gets what they want sexually and who does not. Typically we still live in a male-dominated world. Our businesses, our political and legal systems are all run predominately by men.

Our culture also supports male sexual expression far more than female sexual empowerment.

Consider the following scenario. A couple is having sex. The man is inside the woman and, having orgasmed, rolls over, finishing the sex act. The woman quietly turns over too, despite not having had an orgasm. Even though she might wish for one, she has learned that once the man is done, sex is over. Does this sound familiar to you? Can you admit to having been part of that dynamic, whether as a man or a woman? We would suggest that almost every one of us has been guilty of allowing it at one time or another. Sadly this is all too common an experience for women in our culture.

Now imagine the scenario the other way round: the woman experiences orgasm before the man and rolls over. Can you really see the man turning over and meekly giving up his desire for orgasm? Imagine the woman saying, 'That was great. Good night,' and the man simply accepting this without protest. It seems almost laughable.

What would the man most likely do in such circumstances? Perhaps he would insist on his right to 'finish' the sexual act, ending with his own orgasm. Some men may take matters into their own hands and finish the job themselves. Whatever the method, we can be quite certain that in this scenario a man is unlikely to let his sexual needs go unmet. Of course, we're making generalizations, but why is it that men seem to have a sense of sexual entitlement and many women don't?

Pornography has much to answer for in the insidious messages that it offers. The staple of most male-female pornography is that the woman is there to provide pleasure for the man. Once the man has had his orgasm, her role is fulfilled. Most online pornography ends pretty much as soon as the man has ejaculated. This isn't the only place where we find such sexist messages. Our culture influences the type of pornography that is made and, in turn, the pornography influences how people feel about sexuality. It's a vicious circle.

In this book, we want to help you to overturn such stereotypical behaviours and to help you feel sexually empowered, , whatever your gender.

THE TWO GOLDEN RULES OF SELF-DEVELOPMENT

One of our golden rules for self-development is this simple formula: awareness creates conscious choice, which in turn creates empowerment.

Empowerment doesn't mean having power over others but the power we have over ourselves, our feelings and our behaviours. The purpose of this book is to empower you by helping you to gain a deeper understanding of your own sexuality. Once we start having awareness of our actions and, more importantly, our inactions, we can begin to make conscious choices rather than allowing old patterns to rule our lives. Such choices enable change, growth and, ultimately, ownership of our power and how we choose to express ourselves.

By following the exercises in this book you should gain a far deeper awareness of your own sexuality: what motivates it, your true sexual desires and what obstacles you put in their way – and why. You can then discover the potential of your sexual self and gain a new sense of empowerment, both in relation to your sexuality and in the choices – both conscious and unconscious – you make around relationships, such as the type of partner you engage with and your behaviours within the relationship.

Our other rule for self-development is, 'Be gentle with yourself.' However you feel about yourself at the beginning, the art of any personal growth work is to love yourself more. Yes, there can be a place for self-criticism, for motivating yourself to move forwards and make the necessary changes within yourself. However, usually the most loving thing you can do for yourself is to be gentle. If you take nothing else from this book, learning to be gentler with yourself will be worth the cover price. By loving yourself more, you create more space to be yourself. You offer yourself a greater sense of self-acceptance and it's through this and through self-love that this change can blossom.

USING THIS BOOK

Throughout this book we'll invite you to reflect on what you've read and we suggest you keep a notebook designated for this journey.

We also highly recommend that you take time to do the exercises. Each exercise is part of a guided process, a step-by-step journey, into the heart of your sexual self. You can just read each instruction as you go, or you can download an audio version from our website, www.mazantilousada.com, as we've described on page 47.

In many of the exercises, your eyes will be closed for much the time. If you are referring to the book, don't try to memorize all the instructions beforehand. Instead, once you have closed your eyes to get ready for each step, you can open them just to read the next instruction.

Whatever an exercise reveals about your sexual self, remember it's only a reflection of what your sexuality is today; it's not fixed. Just as your personality changes, so does your sexuality. After all, what's important to you today is unlikely to be what was important to you a decade ago. Similarly, can you remember what mattered to you as a child, perhaps at five or six years old? Was it that trip to the zoo, or the absolute need to get that lollipop? Did such things matter ten years later, when you were a teenager? Perhaps by then it was whether or not a particular boy or girl was interested in you, or whether or not you were popular at school, and so on.

Who we are changes as we move through each phase of life. Even in adulthood our sense of who we are can shift. Perhaps as a younger person you were concerned about outward appearance or career success. As we grow older we tend to find greater satisfaction from our internal space than from outward factors.

Our sexuality, too, is a constantly shifting ocean of possibility. So if you acknowledge things about yourself that make you feel uncomfortable – such as a fantasy you're ashamed of – remember they are only a reflection of where you are now and what is important to you at the moment. As you work on these desires they may transform. The more you can accept your sexuality, the more possibility for pleasure you give yourself. We warmly welcome you on this journey into more authentic, living, breathing, fulfilling sex!

Exercise: Sexual Myths (20 minutes)

From very early on in our lives we absorb messages about our body, our sexuality and about relationships from our family, friends, teachers, society, media imagery and perhaps a religious institution. Typically, as we grow into our teens we will be exposed to pornography. This adds a new set of images to our mental framework for what sex is and what it's supposed to look like. This exercise will help you to understand the early patterning and myths that have impacted your sexuality.

I. Dedicate some time in a quiet space where you won't be disturbed, with notebook and pen close to hand.

2. Take a few moments to connect with yourself by sitting comfortably. Gently close your eyes and turn your awareness to your breathing, taking slow, deep breaths; notice how this helps you to feel your body more. Take a few moments just to enjoy the connection.

3. Now, in your mind's eye, travel back to your childhood and try to see, as vividly as you can, the relationship between your parents or primary caregivers. Did you see them express physical or emotional affection for each other? How was their reaction to other people's sexual or intimate expression (intimacy on TV, public kissing, women in short skirts and so on)?

4. Expand your awareness into the messages you received from older siblings, friends, teachers or anyone else influential in your life as a child and young person. Do any particularly significant memories of your childhood experience of sexuality come to mind? What messages did you pick up about sex, love and intimacy?

5. Now travel to a time when you became aware of the existence of porn. What was your first reaction to porn? What did you learn about sex from being aware of porn?

6. Make some notes about what you've discovered so far in this exercise and consider what sexual myths have formed in your subconscious, based on these initial imprints. Here are some examples you might have learned:

    • To openly display intimacy or desire is 'bad' behaviour

    • If men openly want sex they are 'studs'; if women do, they are 'sluts'

    • Sex is for procreation and only between married couples

    • Men have more desire for sex than women

    • Sex that is not between one man and one woman is perverted

    • Pure sexual desire is morally wrong

    • Sex is dirty

- The bigger the penis the better

- The harder and faster you have sex the better

- Men should always have an erection during sex

- Every woman orgasms from penetrative sex

- Men and women should always be ready for sex

- Orgasm is the goal of sex

- If you have fantasies about sex with someone of the same gender, you must be gay

- If your partner is watching pornography, there must be something wrong with your relationship

What are your personal sexual myths? Write down as truthfully as you can your most deeply engrained beliefs about sex and intimacy, even if they don't feel true anymore or you know they're not true but a part of you still secretly believes them.

7. When you're finished, give yourself some time to sit with this picture of the formative landscape of your sexuality and notice how you feel. We will use this as a kind of road map of your relationship with sex and intimacy. Do you feel embarrassed? Do you laugh at the messages from your childhood? Are there any you would like to challenge or explore, or that make you feel uncomfortable or even provoked?

Understanding these childhood stories is an essential part of the journey into understanding your sexuality as an adult. We'll be exploring this idea more as your journey develops.

The Pros and Cons
of Pornography

Among the ways that sexuality has been hijacked, the most significant include the various media that are available in the technological world. That's not to say that technology is wrong, nor that technology is responsible for the cheapening or shaming of sexuality – this has been going on for thousands of years, before the Internet, before the concept of marketing products and glossy magazines.

The media age brings with it both benefits and problems when it comes to sexuality. In marketing terms, sex sells: any product in the world can be attached to sexual images and made potentially more saleable, more attractive to the consumer. The omnipresence of sexual imagery in both advertising and the media makes sexuality more accessible, more readily brought to mind. However, at the same time this diminishes it, making it less potent than it actually is. By being presented with sexuality on billboards and in magazines or newspapers on a daily basis, we numb ourselves to its true meaning, to its true depth and to its potential in our lives. It ceases to be a gateway to a sacred (though not necessarily religious) relationship with life and instead becomes a commodity, something to be bought and sold, a thing that can be priced rather than valued.

In the digital age, one of the main areas where we see problems arising around our relationship with sexuality is pornography.

Since the emergence of the Internet, our cultural relationship with pornography has changed. Before, if you wanted to see pornography, you had to buy a magazine or covertly rent or buy a video – a purchase usually requiring an interface with another person, i.e. going into a shop to buy the magazine, video and so on, this in itself often a point of shame and embarrassment for many people. However, with the Internet we can all access pornography online in the privacy of our own homes without anyone else (except our search engine) knowing about it, giving us almost unlimited access to sexual imagery. This is both a gift and a burden.

Pornography is a topic about which people get very impassioned; many vilify it, some defend it. Whatever anyone's views on pornography, one thing is certain: easy access to pornography is here to stay. It's as much a part of our modern lives as mobile phones or advertising. It's therefore useful to look at how we can have a more conscious relationship with it, how it can be used to serve us and the problems it can pose.

As psychotherapists, authors of this book and in our non-professional lives, we are not anti-pornography; we believe that pornography is neither good nor bad.

Whether pornography impacts us positively or negatively depends on how we use it and what we make it mean.

When used in moderation and when done so consciously, pornography can offer health benefits, psychological benefits and relational benefits. As the saying goes, a little bit of what you fancy does you good. If pornography stimulates your sexual appetite or increases the range of possibilities of how and why you have sex, then it might add something extra to your sex life and bring a lot of pleasure. It can also be a valid means of stress relief and relaxation, benefiting your psychological wellbeing as well as your relationship.

Concerns around pornography seem to arise from two main issues: how we use it and what we make it mean. The main problem is when pornography is seen not as a means of entertainment or of broadening sexual horizons but as a truth regarding sexuality; when pornography either replaces real, relational sexual experiences or becomes an unconscious norm to which we compare ourselves. A dependence upon pornography can inhibit the user's ability to relate to others in a respectful and connecting manner. A small minority of viewers will watch pornography compulsively and this may affect their capacity to have real-life sexual experiences or even relationships. In this case, the use of pornography becomes an unhealthy pattern that furthers loneliness and isolation.

Other problems arise when people use pornography in secret from their partner to meet sexual needs unfulfilled in their relationship. This may stem from an emotional laziness to address the reason why sex is challenged in the relationship and in this case the use of porn will have a detrimental effect on the couple's emotional wellbeing.

Our male clients who are in this situation often tell us they feel a huge amount of shame and guilt around watching porn behind their partner's back; to them it's a 'dirty secret'. Correspondingly, our female clients might have discovered that their husbands are using porn and will feel hugely rejected, insecure about their bodies, angry towards their husbands and judgmental about their husbands' 'dirty desires'. In this scenario, porn means our sexuality is dirty (traditional male perspective) or that we're not good enough (traditional female perspective). These views make sexual feelings shameful and threatening to the relationship, especially if they are not felt solely around our romantic partner.

Yet for couples there's an immense richness to discover in addressing both their individual and shared sexualities. If both partners can take responsibility for their unmet needs and desires, they can turn the use of porn from something that undermines the relationship into an enriching part of their shared sexuality, even if only one partner actively uses porn to stimulate their sexual response.

But by far the most common problem around pornography is the skewed perspective it gives on sex as the reality or the norm that people need to live up to.

> *It's when pornography sets the standard of what*
> *is normal in sex, what is expected in sex and*
> *what is fashionable, that the problems arise.*

It's when porn becomes so normalized that people believe this is what real-life sex should look like that we lose touch with our natural, healthy, innate, authentic and innocent sexual self-expression. From our client experience, we know this can lead to issues around self-worth, performance, lack of arousal or libido and even aversion to sex.

This belief in the 'reality' of pornography is akin to watching a Hollywood blockbuster then thinking you can go out and perform death-defying stunts. It's like watching a movie featuring an impossibly gorgeous actress with a seemingly 'perfect' body and believing that, as a woman, you should look like that, too. Fortunately, very few people walk out of a Hollywood movie and try to imitate the stunts from the film, but all too many men and women are susceptible to Hollywood body images, believing that these are normal and show how they should look.

Our perception of sex is also impacted by the images we receive; bearing in mind that mainstream media culture is almost clinically void of any imagery that depicts sexual activity (as opposed to its massive use of sexualized seduction), and that we don't have any common, cultural image bank of natural and real sexual expression, the only images that we receive of sex 'in action' are from pornography. This puts porn in a very powerful position.

Sadly but understandably, then, many people who are exposed to pornography come to believe that this is what sex is and this is how they should behave sexually. This is why it's so important to remember that pornography is intended primarily as entertainment, to feed our subconscious with images that stimulate our arousal. It is not real.

THE BENEFITS OF PORNOGRAPHY

There can, however, be benefits from watching pornography. Some of these might come from the act of having an orgasm and others arise simply through the level of arousal and aliveness that is created from watching the material itself.

> *Watching pornography also appears to have*
> *health benefits, especially for men.*

Most people, especially men, watch pornography primarily in order to have an orgasm and ejaculate. A 2003 study, 'Sexual Factors and Prostate Cancer', published in the *British Journal of Urology International* (BJUI) showed that men who ejaculate more than five times a week are less likely to develop prostate cancer: toxins that can cause prostate disease build up in the urogenital tract and by ejaculating men help flush these away. Regular ejaculation also helps to build up your immune system. So regular ejaculation, at least for men – which could come from watching porn – is beneficial to your health. Orgasm also relaxes the body and releases a big hit of positive neurochemicals such as dopamine and oxytocin.

Let's also look at some of the more direct benefits of watching pornography. According to a 2013 study by the Carnegie Mellon University in Pittsburgh, Pennsylvania,[3] watching pornography can reduce the amount of stress hormones in the brain by almost 50 per cent. In the study, co-author Dr J. David Creswell and his team found that watching sexual imagery reduces the brain's amount of cortisol, a hormone released in response to stress and that helps to calm the nervous system. Whilst cortisol isn't bad in itself, continued high levels of it can raise blood sugar, which may cause diabetes, while long-term raised cortisol levels increase blood pressure, suppress digestion and cause insomnia. Which is why having an orgasm when you can't get to sleep is an effective remedy.

Pornography may also act as an effective way to broaden your sexual horizons. By watching new situations and behaviours in pornography you can open your mind to a greater range of sexual possibilities. It can also allow you to explore your sexual fantasies or gain knowledge and information about sexual practices you've been curious about. If these are watched in a way where they won't create further feelings of shame, it can be healing to see that others share these desires and this can help you to come to terms with them. Pornography can help to normalize your desires and fantasies.

Owing to the repressive cultural environment in which we live, a frequent problem with sexuality is that it often gives rise to crippling feelings of shame that lead to self-loathing or self-hatred. We'll explore how to overcome these painful feelings later in the book, including a different and powerful approach to self-healing. However, if using pornography can help to alleviate some of these feelings of shame then it, too, can have a positive impact on your relationship with your sexuality.

> *The occasional use of pornography in a relationship, to help stir things up if libido has dropped away, can be helpful.*

Openly and nonjudgmentally exploring what turns your partner on, through inviting them to share what type of pornography they watch and watching it with them, can provide many of the benefits listed above. Shared use of pornography can help to alleviate shame, create desire and arousal and provide insight into your partner's sexual inner world that they may not have shared with you already. Such use of erotic material can be both healing and transformative in a relationship.

However, dependence on pornography can create problems. Remember that empowerment comes from having greater choice (see this book's 'Introduction'). If using pornography is one of a range of choices to help you get in touch with your sexual energy, this may be empowering for you. If, however, you become dependent upon it, it will not.

WOMEN IN PORNOGRAPHY

It's important to note the difference between the way men and women use porn. Without falling into a gender-stereotypical description, it's fair to say that most porn is produced for, and consumed by, men.

> *In most conventional porn, women*
> *are objectified and cast into a role of*
> *stimulating men's sexual pleasure.*

Even though many shots are focused on the penis and male ejaculation, this is not intended to stimulate women's desire. By keeping the focus on the male experience, conventional porn invites the viewer to identify with the male character of the scenario. Conventional porn, in general, simply displays sex seen from a male perspective.

Many women therefore find it hard to identify with the scenario in a way that stimulates their deeper arousal. The explicit depiction of sex in most porn does not turn them on, simply because their sexuality is different. Again, we're speaking in broad terms, as the difference between 'man' and 'woman' and their respective sexuality is a social construct that does not represent the full range of gender and sexual orientations. However, without wanting to oversimplify the matter, we can say that men's and women's sexuality is different for both biological and sociological reasons.

For men, visual stimulation quickly leads to arousal and with arousal the desire to orgasm. They don't need to think twice if they want it or not. From an evolutionary perspective, it's often argued that men are driven by their desire to spread their genes as widely as possible. Although this argument doesn't allow for multiple other factors, society's norms and values continue to support it by valuing male sexual potency.

Women's sexuality is somewhat more complex. Women tend to need a higher degree of erotic 'storytelling' to identify with a sexual scenario. They usually need intimate connection, foreplay and presence. Presence is our ability to feel, sense and acknowledge our own sensations, emotions and thoughts as well as other people's; it's our ability to be in connection with our environment (including other people) and ultimately to have a meaningful impact upon it.

> *Compared to men's visual stimulation, women are, in general, more aroused by a combination of touch and presence.*

From an evolutionary perspective, the argument is that women need to consider whether or not their partner is able to look after them and their children when sabre-toothed tigers are lurking, and this makes connection and intimacy more important in women's arousal pattern.

Of course, male and female sexualities are far more complex than this and are driven by many factors besides evolution. However, for a wide range of social, ideological and biological reasons, these ideas have been perfectly adapted into the social norm that 'good girls don't want sex just for the sake of it'. Female sexual expression is defined by a range of social control mechanisms that ensure a woman doesn't get 'carried away' by sexual desire. Women have simply learned to suppress their sexuality and to think that it's defined by a sole male partner. For this reason, many women have an indifferent or even negative reaction to porn, according to how strong their social conditioning has been.

This can very often lead to women's shaming or judgment of their men if they discover them watching porn. It's a situation in which a woman's judgment of porn equals her relationship with her own sexuality. Her view of explicit sex as 'bad' and shameful mirrors the belief she has unconsciously learned from others – that her own sexuality is bad and shameful. This would explain why she might unconsciously feel resentful that he can have something that she can't. The fact that she might not be turned on by the same kind of imagery as her partner does not mean anything other than that she needs to bring her own desires to the relationship.

In many cases, sadly, this is part of the problem. As a result of society's suppressive norms about female sexuality, women have largely declined from being more biologically receptive into being socially passive. They've learned to disown their sexuality to a point where they don't really know what turns them on, thus projecting their disowned sexuality onto their partner and perceiving it as 'bad' sexuality.

> *A partner's use of porn can feel like betrayal; that they are unfaithful because they prefer to watch porn instead of having sex as a couple.*

While this might be the case in relationships where emotional blocks have come between the couple's sexual desire for each other, it's important to remind ourselves that our partners' substitution of porn for sex is a wake-up call for both parties that the dynamic between the couple isn't flowing freely. It might show as a symptom in sex, but it's most likely to reflect a much more general difficulty. If the sexual aliveness gained from watching porn is taken back into the relationship, to reawaken or stimulate the couple's sex, it's an entirely positive and healthy thing for both partners.

Like everything else concerning our real sexual desires, the more we can be ourselves in the relationship, the less we have to feel shameful about who we are and the more the relationship will thrive and grow. If a partner's use of porn is accepted and supported, they will be able to bring back into the relationship what porn gives them. If they have to keep it secret, it will further the distance between the couple. As we'll see in the chapter 'Authentic Communication' (see page 147), open communication is an absolute key to 'real sex'.

PORN AND OUR ANIMALISTIC NATURE

Fortunately, this old paradigm of men using porn and women resenting it seems to be changing rapidly.

There is a small but growing amount of pornography made by women for women.

In such erotic material men's pleasure is not the predominant focus and the woman is rarely seen as objectified. More time is typically spent on the sensual awakening of those involved and penetrative sex takes up less screen time than in conventional pornography.

However, the majority of pornography is still made by men for men. It carries the old-style patriarchal attitude that women are less important than men. Women in pornography are frequently objectified and seem simply to exist in order to provide men with sexual stimulus and pleasure. The women's own needs and desires are given little importance. Such denigration and objectification belittles women and offers the suggestion that it's acceptable to treat women in this degrading manner. Naturally, many women and men feel emotionally appalled by pornography for this reason.

While porn's gender dynamic is of course unacceptable and unrepresentative in real life, let's remind ourselves again that porn is not real. It offers imagery that stimulates our arousal and sexual response.

At a deeper level we could say that the majority of pornography speaks to our animalistic nature.

Desire for raw, unfiltered sexual expression, with no connection, no attachment and no sensitivity to relationship or gender equality, is a part of our animalistic nature and survival instinct, whether we can accept this within ourselves and take responsibility for this impulse, or not. In other words, can we own this desire or do we disown it? The more we disown it, of course, the more likely we are to vilify it.

Over thousands of years of patriarchy, women have learned to deny their animalistic nature and to cultivate their emotional nature. As a result, their own inner masculinity – that sexually raw and objectifying part of them – has been denied. In this sense, as we mentioned at the beginning of this chapter, porn is neither good nor bad. It's how we use it and what we make it mean that can impact us either positively or negatively. Porn itself simply offers us access to aspects of our free, unfiltered sexuality and animalistic nature that the majority of people normally suppress because these things are judged as culturally unacceptable. In this sense, porn in itself can be seen as positive and healthy, because it helps us to embrace the whole spectrum of our humanness.

It's when we forget that most porn is seen from a male perspective, and when we judge our animalistic nature, that porn can have a negative impact on our sexuality.

Further problems arise when we believe that porn is real and when we start using it as inspiration for our sexuality.

This may sound very obvious, but sadly porn imagery has insidiously infiltrated itself deeply into our collective consciousness in the way many of us think and feel about sex. The fact that sexual expression is still covered by layers of taboo and silence, even in sex education, not to mention general, public imagery, means we have nowhere to turn when we want to learn about sex 'in action'. Pornography, then, inadvertently becomes the image bank available to us, and if we use it without being conscious of its limitations porn very easily becomes the equivalent of 'normal' sex, the 'truth' about sex. Even if we don't actively use it, if porn represents 'sex' in our minds our sexuality will be affected.

'Real sex' offers an antidote to this limited perspective, not by banning porn but by offering a different perspective on sexuality. We'll help you discover for yourself what sex means to you, what turns you on and what your authentic desires are. We'll invite men and, especially, women (since we more often experience them in our client practice as sexually disowned) to step more fully and authentically into their sexual selves, and to teach their partners to communicate clearly and respectfully.

For now, however, let's have a look at the ways porn imagery has impacted our society in the way we think and feel about sex.

PORNOGRAPHY AND BODY IMAGE

The strongest impact pornography has on society is not the frequent guilt and shaming that surrounds the use of porn (especially in monogamous, heterosexual relationships) – it's that much pornography subtly creates a skewed perspective on what is important in sex. Through pornography we have images in our minds that we think we need to repeat in reality. This can be potentially damaging to our body image, to our actual experience of pleasure, to how we relate to our partners and our sense of self-worth.

We know that most porn is made for men by men. Women's pleasures seem to be given little importance apart from orgasms, which are mostly faked in order to stir men's pleasure.

Women are objectified and behave in ways that facilitate men's, and not their own, pleasure.

For instance, there's a strong tendency to portray women as having an endless willingness to be instantly available for any type of sex, including anal sex without any apparent lubrication. This depiction of women is largely inaccurate and potentially painful for women trying to emulate this act in real life.

A seemingly constant readiness for sex is not the only pressure women tend to feel when comparing themselves to pornography. For example, we may also infer from pornography that all women are interested in a same-sex experience. In reality, only 11 per cent of women have had a same-sex experience (although this number is growing for both sexes) and fewer than 40 per cent have tried anal sex.[4]

There's also a strong tendency for pornography to favour actresses who have little or no visible inner labia on the vulva. A 2013 report from the Royal College of Obstetricians and Gynaecologists[5] claimed that the digital or cosmetic modification of images of women's bodies in pornography is leading to an increase in cosmetic genital surgery.

Although the report also cites physical discomfort and possible hygiene issues as reasons for having larger labia reduced in size, it stresses that the primary reason women ask for a labiaplasty (a surgical procedure to cut back the inner labia) is their concern about their physical appearance.

Labiaplasty is big business and growing fast. In 2013 the NHS performed over 2,000 labiaplasties, five times as many as it performed in 2008. However, since the majority of labiaplasties are performed privately, it's hard to get a measure of how many operations are undertaken in the UK each year. The actual number of labiaplasties performed in the UK is, then, likely to be far higher and with the average cost at £3,500, labiaplasty represents huge profits for those who offer the procedure. This may be a major factor in surgeons' decision to do so.

The majority of women asking for labiaplasty are under the age of 30, and having learned from pornography that their labia are 'supposed' to look neat and symmetrical, sadly become convinced that there's something wrong with them 'down there'. In reality this is untrue.

The size, colour and shape of inner labia vary from woman to woman as widely as any other body part, such as breast size, nose shape or hair colour.

In any case, about half of women have inner labia that are larger than their outer labia. So either way, whether your labia protrude or they don't, you are normal. It's also normal for one inner labia to be larger than the other. This does not mean there is anything wrong with you. It's simply anatomical variation and part of the beautiful spectrum of female genitals, just as there are differences in penis size, girth and shape.

It's disturbing, then, when partners – usually male – make a derogatory comment about a woman's labia, their judgment being based on the artificial imagery they've seen in pornography. Such comments are not only insensitive but also potentially traumatic for a woman, especially if she does not have much sexual experience or self-confidence.

There also appears to be a more worrying trend in much pornography: for female porn actresses to have little or no pubic hair. Too often we hear stories, especially from younger women, of their male partners refusing to 'go down' on them unless they shave off their pubic hair. It is for women themselves to define their relationship with their genitals, not the attempts of their partners or a male-dominated media to dictate this.

This trend for hairless vulvas with smaller labia potentially has a darker side. Young girls do not, typically, have large inner labia; the labia grow as a woman matures and comes into her adult body. Nor do young girls have pubic hair. A hairless vulva with non-visible or small inner labia could therefore be said to emulate an immature female body, a child-like quality that disempowers women and, worse still, creates an implicit message about the desirability of young girls as opposed to sexually mature women.

Women's concerns about their labia are not the only body issues that pornography creates. Porn can create an unrealistic perception of men's bodies as well as women's. Male porn performers are often chosen simply for the size of their penis. The average penis in pornography measures 7–9 inches in length. In real life, the average Caucasian penis measures five-and-a-half inches, with the average African-Caribbean penis half an inch longer and the average Asian penis half an inch shorter. After viewing pornography, this leaves many men feeling inadequate in that department, which can lead to many issues such as erectile problems and self-worth issues.

For women, it's not just their labia that they might compare unfavourably with porn actresses'. Porn breasts are typically large and pert, often with artificial surgical help. Most porn actresses, at least in mainstream pornography, have a certain body type that is an exaggerated mirror of the media portrayal of the 'perfect' female form: large breasts, firm bottom and slim waist. Both pornography and, more broadly, media culture clearly create pressure on women to conform to this one specific type of beauty, leaving those whose bodies do not fit within its narrow criteria often feeling inadequate and with strong feelings of self-loathing for their bodies that is a guaranteed route to losing libido.

We will help you overcome these feelings of insecurity about your body with exercises that allow you to begin to truly love your body as it is.

Feeling inadequate when comparing oneself to pornography is not limited to physical attractiveness. Pornography pays little attention to the subtleties and feelings of the sexual act and concentrates far more on the performance of sex, particularly orgasm – both for men and for women.

> **The constant focus on orgasm – especially, for men, of ejaculation – makes it appear that it's the goal of sex.**

Yet for men, premature ejaculation is the number-one issue for which they seek sexual help or advice. This very often arises from self-imposed performance pressure, often associated with gaining false expectations by watching pornography.

And while women in pornography appear to be able to orgasm easily through penetration alone, in reality around 75 per cent of women have never experienced orgasm this way. Studies also show that about 30–35 per cent of women have never experienced any form of orgasm.[6] Fortunately, while orgasm is a pleasurable experience, it doesn't have to be the point of sex. Among the benefits of 'real sex' is that it doesn't follow this orgasm-centric model of sexuality, yet it allows you to both increase your sexual pleasure and extend your sexual experiences.

Pornography also suggests that men should be able to have endless vigorous penetrative sex and remain constantly hard throughout any sexual experience. In reality, most men ejaculate within three minutes of penetrative sex and it's natural in the course of a longer sexual experience that the penis will grow or shrink depending on what is happening at that moment.

> *The idea that the man's penis must remain constantly*
> *hard – and if it doesn't there's something wrong with*
> *him – is a myth created largely by pornography.*

This usually self-imposed pressure has led many men to become anxious about the strength of their erections. Ironically, one of the fastest ways to lose an erection is to worry about it, so this rapidly becomes a vicious circle: more anxiety about erections creates more problems with erections.

But by taking the focus away from performance and towards pleasure, a different model of sexuality can help men and women to relax, enjoy their sexual experience more and let go of their anxieties around it. This is what you get with 'real sex'.

Unfortunately the pharmaceutical industry has in the meantime exploited this vulnerability and anxiety in men, and pills such as Viagra and Cialis are a multi-billion-dollar industry. In some cases, pharmacological help is invaluable, but in many instances the issues are psychological and based on performance-based fears rather than hormonal or physiological issues.

A recent trend in pornography is that of female ejaculation, or 'squirting'. While this is a genuine and scientifically documented phenomenon, the majority of female ejaculation in pornography is faked. Although, as experienced therapists, we believe that every woman has the ability to ejaculate, the proportion of women who regularly do so is just 6 per cent.[7]

Whilst female ejaculation is a beautiful thing both to experience and to witness as a partner, the feeling that it's some kind of novelty or circus trick that a woman is required to perform on demand creates a new type of pressure on women. Even if a partner is skilled at helping a woman to ejaculate, the feeling that he or she is expecting the woman to squirt not only creates performance pressure but is also a subtle form of objectification. It's as though the woman becomes a toy with the ability to squirt, or simply orgasm, in order to assuage the partner's ego.

> ### *The fascination with female ejaculation in pornography is perhaps a subtle way in which the woman is made to be more like the man in sex.*

Her ejaculation becomes a mirror of the male orgasmic release, allowing the predominately male viewers to relate to her in a new way.

Female ejaculation has become popular in pornography partly because it can be seen. A woman's moans of orgasmic pleasure – usually badly faked for the cameras – have become insufficient to satisfy viewers' appetite for visual climax to a pornographic movie. Pornographic sex is therefore about what is visible, about what the camera can pick up, rather than any subtler interplay between those involved. Consequently there's a predisposition towards 'hard-pounding' sex where the penis is vigorously thrust into the vagina, anus or mouth; pornography creates the myth that 'bigger cocks, banging harder, make for better sex'. Less obvious movements such as a rotation of the pelvis in penis-to-vagina sex don't show up so well on camera so they are largely ignored. Whilst hard sex can be pleasurable, if that is your definition of what makes good sex it's extremely limiting. By contrast, the subtleties of 'real sex' create greater sexual intensity and more pleasure for all involved.

University of Cambridge research in 2014 that studied the effects of pornography on the brain mentioned earlier also found that 50 per cent of its subjects, whose average age was 25, suffered from erectile problems in real life but not when viewing pornography.[8] This may suggest that issues of performance arose when faced with the challenge of interacting on a sexual level with a real human being, while erotic stimuli from pornography create no such problems. Although the jury is still out on this, it seems possible that pornography is partly responsible for a generation of young men and women who are less able to interact at the deeper levels of intimacy that a meaningful interpersonal sexual experience invites us to explore. Consequently they are retreating further from real-world relations into a world of virtual sex.

A recent study by the Japan Family Planning Association showed that the country's under-forties are losing their interest not only in sex but also in dating in general.[9] The issue has become so prevalent that the Japanese media even has a name for it: *sekkusu shinai shokugun*, or celibacy syndrome. The 2013 survey found that 45 per cent of women aged 16–24 'weren't interested in, or despised, sexual contact'. Just over a quarter of men felt the same way. Of course, the use of pornography may be only one of many factors contributing to this decline in sexual self-expression but, for Japan at least, the numbers are clearly significant.

THE QUESTION OF PORN ADDICTION

As well as the issues around some of the personal and relational problems that using porn can cause, there's also concern around 'porn addiction'. While the existence of porn addiction hasn't been confirmed, the 2014 Cambridge study (see page 39) suggested there is some evidence that compulsively watching pornography can lead to an addiction to porn. The study showed that compulsive porn users craved more porn but this didn't lead to higher levels of desire for sex with another person. In effect, the study observed, they became hooked on watching porn but not on having sex in the real world. This has been likened to a drug user wanting more of the drug but not enjoying it.

The study took a control group of 'normal' individuals and tested them against a group of compulsive porn users. This seems to demonstrate the potential for porn addiction in those who are predisposed to compulsive behaviour. This is not necessarily an indicator that the average porn viewer would become addicted.

It seems that porn addiction is less about addiction and more about compulsive behaviour.

Watching pornography or masturbating may also become a compulsion similar to Obsessive Compulsive Disorder (OCD). If there's an overwhelming sense of needing to watch pornography to a point where it interferes with an individual's capacity to carry on with their normal life – to hold down a job, to have a healthy relationship or to enjoy real-world sexual experiences – this is clearly detrimental and it's highly advisable that they seek support in one form or another.

For some people, applying the label of an 'addict' is counter-productive and may provide an excuse for their inappropriate behaviour, simply saying, 'I can't help it: I'm an addict.' However, for others, labelling themselves a porn addict can be reassuring and will give them a sense that they are not alone. Organizations such as Sex Addicts Anonymous or Sex and Love Addicts Anonymous help many people by offering a path out of dependency and by providing a support network of like-minded individuals who are sharing a common journey. Many others find support through psychotherapy, counselling, spiritual groups or other support networks, or simply by talking to their partner or friends.

WHEN WE BELIEVE IN PORN

So, porn in itself is neither good nor bad. In general, it simply represents a raw aspect of sexuality – predominately male. Understood in this way, it can provide pleasure as well as health and sexual benefits for its users and their partners. Problems arise when porn becomes the main way to express oneself sexually, or when it becomes the model for sexual expression around which we form our sexual identity. This is what we're seeing in those – particularly the under-thirties – who have grown up with the availability of online pornography that was absent in previous generations.

Porn, then, has an enormous capacity to affect our body image and self-image, and to influence the way we think we ought to have sex.

*Porn has put both men and women under pressure
to perform, the most profound impact of which is
that we lose connection with our own pleasure.*

Sexual performance has become a yardstick for whether or not we are 'successful' in sex. The importance we place on performance makes us stay locked in our heads and out of touch with what our bodies are actually feeling.

When we're out of our bodies, we also lose touch with who we are sexually.

This is the simplest but most profound message of 'real sex'.

Additionally, while porn is usually seen from the limited and stereotypically male perspective and women's sexual response is generally stirred not by visual stimulation but by touch and presence, female sexuality remains misrepresented in porn. Most women won't recognize themselves in porn but nor will they find an alternative with a positive representation of their sexuality. The messages about their sexuality they've received from parents, church or society will largely be that 'good girls don't have sex' and therefore their sexuality remains unowned.

This is one of the most important areas of growth in contemporary society. As long as female sexuality remains unowned, women will continue to project potency, power and, ultimately, aggression onto men, who will be caught in this projection, unable to unlock their sensitivity, and women will remain passive and resentful. Neither men nor women will be able to access a place where they can be both sensitive and potent, which is ultimately reflected in society as a whole.

*One of the most fascinating things about sex
is that it's a microcosm of societal values.*

So, is porn wrong? Should governments try to censor and limit its distribution, as the UK has in recent years? The majority of porn offers a distorted view of sex, but that doesn't mean porn should be vilified. It's not a ban of online pornography that we need, but an altogether new representation of sexuality within it. New types of imagery, language and perspective are required for men and women to have a healthier relationship with both pornography and, more fundamentally, with their sexuality within society. This includes the need for more pornography that comes not from the old paradigm of masculine power and female submission or servitude, but from a new perspective of the empowered feminine as well as a more present masculine.

THE
SEVEN KEYS
TO
REAL SEX

In the following chapters, we will explain the Seven Keys to 'real sex', including exercises you can do on your own or with a partner. We recommend that before you do each exercise, you read from the start of the chapter in which it's given.

Audio tracks

You can download a free audio track with instructions for each exercise from our website: www.mazantilousada.com

Click on the 'REAL SEX' link and enter the password *intimate*.

Exercises using the book alone

If you do the exercises following instructions from the book alone, you can take it step by step, reading each instruction as you go – you don't need to read through the whole exercise beforehand.

KEY 1:
UNDERSTAND
YOUR DESIRE

L et's start this chapter with some seemingly simple questions. What is sex? Why do you want to have sex? What is the nature of desire? If we're going to look at the nature of our desires, it is important that we understand such foundational principles. However, their answers are more complex than they may first appear.

CULTURAL EXPECTATIONS VS AUTHENTIC DESIRE

The answers we first give to these questions are usually the ones that come from what we've been taught to believe. These belief systems may come from our family, our peers, the culture in which we live, the strata of society we inhabit, our religious or spiritual environment, our schools and teachers. Now, more than ever before, each of us is also constantly bombarded with media messages in magazines, newspapers, advertising and, in a less pervasive but equally compelling way, pornography – whether direct or indirect, hardcore or soft and implicit, as increasingly used in advertising. We absorb this continual, often subliminal, messaging no matter how much we might tell ourselves that we don't want to be subjected to it. It's an inevitable byproduct of modern life.

Given all these implicit, and sometimes explicit, influences, it's reasonable to assume that until we really examine them, our beliefs about sexuality are more likely to reflect others' views on sexuality than our own. This is especially true when it comes to messages received in our childhood. It's in these early formative years, when we first learn about sex and sexuality, that our strongest imprints of what we 'ought' to believe are laid down. As children – and very often even as adults – we have a tendency to accept unquestioningly the beliefs we're told without properly analysing and exploring them to see if they hold true for us. These beliefs usually have a significant impact on our sexuality unless we consciously choose to shift them towards something different.

Problems tend to arise when our own
internal desires are in conflict with the
beliefs we've learned from others.

What if our sexuality is different from what we learned is 'normal' in the messages we received? What if we've been told that sex before marriage is wrong but we feel desire for someone without wanting to marry them? What if same-sex attraction is 'wrong' but we feel it anyway? What if we desire a type of sex that we've learned isn't 'okay'? What happens when we have a desire to explore kink or fetish practices, or if we have 'illicit' fantasies such as being with more than one sexual partner or being forced to have sex?

We may feel equally challenged if we can't really feel our sexual desires. Modern culture, especially pornography, emphasizes the expectation to be sexual and to demonstrate a willingness to be sexually available. We may think we ought to feel sexy but we simply cannot find that place within ourselves. We may not know how to feel, be or act sexually.

Many people, therefore, find themselves locked in a struggle between contemporary media culture and the residues of religious and cultural imprinting; expected to feel constantly turned on and ready for sex yet at the same time held back by the taboo of their innate sexual drive.

Unless we choose to engage with it consciously, our natural desire will often be severely coloured by this fear of being either 'too much' or 'not enough'. We're likely to experience this as a disconnect or lack of harmony between the beliefs we learned (often as children), what we think is expected of us and what feels like our own 'truth'.

> *Internal conflict between what we*
> *want and what we think we ought to*
> *want can be profoundly painful.*

A significant step to having 'real sex' is to understand your desires, to allow them to 'be' and to accept them as natural and healthy. Fundamentally, the beliefs we've absorbed from others are unlikely to reflect a true picture of our own sexual desires.

If we continue to believe that other people's pictures of sexuality are a mirror of our own desires, we're likely to be limiting our capacity for sexual pleasure through a broader range of experiences. By realizing that our beliefs about sex are most likely coloured by our culture's mixed messages about what we ought to feel, we can begin to clear the table in order to find out what holds the truth for us.

We'll look at this more in the chapter 'Giving Permission' (see page 171).

WHAT IS SEX?

So, looking at the most basic of our questions, what is sex? When we ask clients in our practice this question we find the range of answers is strikingly diverse. The most common response is that sex consists of penis-in-vagina penetration. For other people it includes certain types of other genital contact, such as oral sex or stimulation of the genitals with fingers or toys. Very often the perception of sex is focused predominately on the genitals and has a tendency to ignore the rest of the body. This means that contact or stimulation of anything other than the genitals is seen as either a waste of time or simply a necessary preamble to the 'main event': penetration or genital contact.

But before rushing straight towards the genitals for arousal, it's important to remember that we also have a whole range of other body parts that can experience pleasure and erotic charge. To ignore them would not only be to limit our experience of pleasure but also to limit what we define as sex.

There can also be confusion between sex and nudity. Some people would say that nudity, or at least partial nudity, was necessary for sex. Another idea seems to be that if we take off our clothes we're going to have sex. It's almost as though we can't be trusted to be naked without such primal urges taking over. Many parts of Europe, such as Germany and Scandinavia, have a more relaxed attitude to nudity, allowing mixed-gender saunas and other nude recreation spaces. In countries such as the UK and the USA there's such confusion between nudity and sex that mixed-gender nudity is heavily discouraged or banned. It's important to examine these two different topics so that we can realize it's possible to be naked without having sex and, similarly, we can have sex without needing to remove clothing.

As an example, you may have been in a club or bar where you've had contact with someone, or seen other people engaging, in ways that are extremely sexual but without anyone undressing. If you tend to get jealous, it might be easiest for you to imagine your partner here. You can probably imagine ways in which they might behave on the dance floor that didn't involve nudity but which you would interpret as being highly sexual and that you wouldn't feel comfortable about.

In fact, it's possible in 'real sex' to experience sex and full-body orgasm without even needing to touch one another, whether clothed or not, simply by connecting with the sexual energy between you so, again, neither nudity nor physical contact is necessary for something to be felt as sex.

Many people have what are often referred to as fetishes, where an object or event holds a strong erotic charge. Take the example of a foot or shoe fetish. For such people, the thought of licking someone's feet or shoes is enough to create not only strong desire and arousal but even an orgasmic response. Similarly, many people experience sexual arousal through contact with other activities such as spanking, whipping or being tied up. To some these acts may be of no interest or repellent but to others these are highly sexual activities. Many people visit sex clubs or professional sex workers to allow themselves to have an experience where there's no direct skin contact or stimulation but where the participants become highly turned on.

The point here is that there is no definition of what sex is, except whatever we think it is. A similar view was famously pronounced by Justice Potter Stewart in Ohio during a 1960s legal case to judge whether the French film *The Lovers* (*Les Amants*) should be banned in the state on the grounds that it was obscene because it was pornographic. He noted:

> *I shall not today attempt further to define the kinds of material*
> *I understand to be embraced within that shorthand description*
> *[in that case 'hard-core' pornography]; and perhaps I could never*
> *succeed in intelligibly doing so. But I know it when I see it.*
> Jacobellis vs Ohio, 1964

Perhaps this is the most reasonable definition of sex. We've seen that for different people sex involves different, wide-ranging and seemingly unrelated activities – so many that it becomes impossible to define sex itself as an activity. Rather, sex is about the energy, intention and reasons behind the activity. Sex, therefore, becomes less about what we do and more about how and why we do it.

Sex is a particular type or quality of energy that we all know when we feel it.

We might also apply this description to orgasm – a description that's infinitely more accurate than the clinical description of a simple ejaculatory release or the contraction of certain pelvic-floor muscles and the vasodilation of some blood vessels. We'll discuss this further in the chapter 'Pleasure, Not Performance' (see page 195).

SEX IS AN ENERGY – SENSUAL VS SEXUAL

In order to explore the 'quality' of sex – the energy that we engage with and the reason we desire certain sexual experiences – we need to consider how sex is felt and experienced in the body.

Sex is an energy that is experienced over time, as a process. We move through different sensations and stages between not feeling sexual at all to feeling highly aroused or ready to peak. This, however, is only what happens in the mind, how the mind interprets a bodily impulse – we notice a certain quality of desire felt in the body then assess whether we want to allow it to expand or not, depending on whether the impulse and circumstances are appropriate. Very often this happens at an unconscious level, so it's our mood, mind and internal beliefs about sex that determine whether we allow the desire to fully arise or not, whether to allow ourselves to access the energy.

The point is that sexual energy is a dormant energy that has no beginning and no end. It just is.

Sexual energy is our life-force energy.

It flows in our bodies as naturally as our hearts beat and our organs function. The question is, do we allow ourselves to feel the energy, to let it access our conscious mind? When do we stop our life-force energy and edit it out? How much sex can we take before we start editing our experience? Where is our threshold?

It's important to understand that as sexual energy is our life-force energy, we can consciously connect to it in each and every moment. It's there already, waiting to be accessed, felt and expressed.

It's this vital body-mind relationship that is core to 'real sex'.

Sex is such a variety of activities but they all share one thing: the energy that arises in us, the felt experience. As mentioned earlier, this energy can move from not being felt at all to being highly charged.

How does his happen? How do we create the flow of desire that allows us to experience sex as a process, happening over time? The clue is to look at the difference between *sensual* energy and *sexual* energy. These are separate yet closely linked energies and both are vitally important in the understanding of our desire.

Sensual energy refers to the experience arising from our senses – from smell, touch, taste, sound and a felt sense. Sensuality is a whole-body experience, in that all body parts and all senses are able to experience pleasure, and a sensual experience is defined by a general feeling of wellbeing.

> *Because sensuality arises from the senses,*
> *it's experienced in the moment and is an*
> *experience with no urge to 'go anywhere'.*

This is why we can be sensual where sexual energy would be inappropriate: cuddly with our friends, children and pets. In relation to others, sensual energy is therefore first and foremost a connective energy. It brings us into an embodied presence with the other (our partner), which creates a sense of wellbeing. Neurologically, our parasympathetic nervous system is activated, making us feel relaxed, loving and open.

Sexual energy is very different. Although it can be felt in the whole body, it has a specific focus that gives it a particular quality. This focus is mainly felt in the genitals and attention keeps returning here even though other body parts can also be stimulated. In addition, sexual energy is innately charged with an increasing intensity. Sexual energy gives us the feeling that it wants to go somewhere; it wants to peak in the orgasm and discharge the energy. Compared to sensual energy as embodied presence, sexual energy feels much more goal-oriented. In essence, it's a drive – it's the life-force energy, which wants to express itself. At that moment, connection and wellbeing become secondary to the urge for the ultimate pleasure. It can feel as though something – the energy itself – is taking over. We surrender, ultimately, to the orgasm, and in that we surrender to something greater, more powerful, than ourselves.

As we define it, real, fulfilling sex consists of an interplay between sensual and sexual energies. It's both embodied presence with the other and life-force energy wanting to express itself in the ultimate surrender. If we think that sex is purely about genital contact until we orgasm, we get trapped in an oversimplified idea of sex – this is what pornography does. Ultimately this deprives us from the pleasure and energetic connection that is experienced in the moment. By consisting of both sensual and sexual energies, sex can be a full-body, connective experience of flow. For this to happen, we need to allow sensual and sexual energies to arise and be expressed.

> *Sensuality gives us the connectivity and*
> *sexuality gives us the urge to surrender.*

This is where the interplay between body and mind is interesting. As we feel desire arising in the body, our mind assesses how much connectivity or surrender we can allow ourselves to experience in any given moment. In understanding our desire, we need to understand that sensual and sexual energies are both part of our sexual expression. Which one do we feel comfortable with and which one would we like to express more fully?

SEX IS NOT LINEAR

Sex, then, is more about how and why we do what we do, and consists of both sensual and sexual energies. Limiting the definitions of sex, whether they arise from our internal judgments or from learned social norms, limits our understanding of what we allow sex to be and therefore restricts the possibilities of what might give us sexual pleasure. So you should hold on only lightly to any preconceived notions you may have about sex because they're likely to stop you from seeing, feeling and experiencing sexuality outside the narrow confines of that understanding.

The broader we can allow our definition of sex to become, the more we can understand that sex is not a linear process. Many people believe that sex begins with foreplay, moves towards penetration and ends with orgasm. This is what we typically see in porn. Orgasm, at least for a man, is usually seen as the end of the movie; the male ejaculation, known as 'the money shot' in porn, is literally the climax of the film. (If a male porn performer doesn't ejaculate, he doesn't get paid.) This can give the impression that sex is supposed to lead towards orgasm, as its natural conclusion.

This limiting belief restricts our ability to understand what is sexual and what our desire actually is. It's common to believe that sex is 'supposed' to move in one direction until the energy is spent, and then we can rest. It's almost as though, when we begin to feel sexual energy, we make a judgment that the energy is supposed to increase in intensity, that the corresponding actions and behaviours should similarly increase in intensity, that 'pressure', if you like, builds up until something explodes, usually in the form of one or both partners having an orgasm.

This linear idea of sex limits our capacity to experience sex as a natural flow of energy in our body system. Instead, allow sex to be whatever you feel and wish to express in each moment, with yourself or another. It may be that an experience begins with holding and cuddling, that it moves towards gentle caresses and soft, tender kissing. The energy may then become sensual for a time. From here it may move into a more sexual quality that may lead to passionate kissing and maybe genital-focused expression or back to more holding and a softer, loving energy.

The point is that there is no right way to have sex.

***There is no defined or required linear sequence
of events or actions that makes for good sex.***

In one moment the quality of the energy may be one thing, which may in turn lead to a shift into another type of energy; or it may not.

Both are okay. If we return to the question of what your desire is, it's important to understand that whatever your authentic desire in each moment, it's okay as long as it's healthily expressed (a subject we'll explore shortly). It's simply energy moving through your system, wanting to be expressed.

Sex is unlike many other activities, which we do for their outcome: making something, working, exercising, cooking and so on. Ideally, sex is something that we do just for the sake of doing it. Just as with making music or dancing, the point is not to finish as fast as possible but to enjoy the journey through the experience. Only rarely is the joy of a piece of music that it gets faster and faster until it reaches a crescendo then comes to a sudden end. This might be pleasing sometimes but if all music were like this we would quickly become bored of it. Some pieces of music increase in tempo, some slow down; symphonies have fast and slow movements interspersed.

There's no right way to compose music, just as there's no right way to have sex.

What makes a piece of music pleasing is the flow of one movement into another. That transition may be gentle and smooth, with the pace gradually increasing or mellowing, or it may comprise a sudden shift from one key to another, creating a contrast in experience that gives a sudden delight.

So it is with sex. It's the flow between qualities of touch or connection, the shift between feeling our otherness and the melting-into-oneness, or the changing of pace from fast to slow and back again, that creates a pleasurable variety of sensation that makes for good sex.

Now we can clear up another myth: orgasm is not the goal of sex.

If that were true, the people who were able to orgasm the most quickly would be considered the best at sex. This is clearly not the case.

Orgasm is simply one of the many sexual experiences. Admittedly it's normally a particularly pleasurable experience, but it need not hold any greater significance than any other part of a sexual engagement and it's certainly not a measure of anything.

WHY DO YOU WANT TO HAVE SEX ANYWAY?

Having redefined sex not as an act but as a quality of energy, as a 'how' not a 'what', we must look at why we wish to experience that energy in the first place. What is it that motivates us to have sex? Understanding this will help you to get a clearer picture of what kind of sex you want to have and what your desires are.

The most basic and culturally acceptable reason for having sex is for its biological function, that of procreation. This is still the underlying philosophy for how our medical world approaches what are labelled as 'sexual dysfunctions', namely erectile dysfunction, orgasmic issues, genital pain and so on. All are concerned with whether penetration can be performed and whether orgasm can be achieved. Conventional sex therapy also arises, for the most part, out of the medical model and tends to look at resolving dysfunction rather than supporting clients to move towards pleasure.

This attitude can also be seen in sex education in schools, where the focus is on avoiding the 'dangers' of sex: sexually transmitted infections (STIs) and pregnancy. In both areas, sexual pleasure for its own sake is either toned down or ignored. There's very little public acknowledgment and guidance in this area. As therapists, our view is that we don't really have 'sex education' in the UK, only what might as well be called 'reproduction education'.

If, then, the social focus is on avoiding 'problems', what happens to sexual pleasure itself? How are we to feel about our desire to have sex for its own sake? For as long as we don't discuss our pleasure and desire openly and authentically, they will remain driven by either the fear-based narratives or another cultural assumption – that if we're in a relationship, we should want to have sex only with our partner and not with anyone else; in other words, by the confinement of a conventional, monogamous relationship. This puts our internal, felt experience of sexual desire under huge pressure: we're not really allowed to discuss it.

There's an expectation that we feel desire, but only with and for our partner.

This means our sexual desire isn't simply flowing freely in its natural expression.

A complex range of internal agendas is involved when we start to shed light on to our reasons to have sex. Some of these we can admit to, others we've unconsciously edited out from our immediate awareness.

For example, many say that sex for pleasure is the most common reason they have sex. This can be so they can feel sexy and alive in themselves; as a stress-reducing, orgasmic release of bodily tension; to feel the physical and emotional closeness of their partner; or it can encompass a wide range of sexual practices that stimulate more unconscious needs, such as the thrill of taboo, kink practices or sexual affairs.

On the other hand, many people within conventional relationships have sex because they feel they ought to – it is, they feel, what is expected of them and it becomes a way to keep the relationship stable. This is usually – though not always – the view of a woman in a heterosexual, monogamous relationship, where the husband or male partner appears to have the greater sex drive.

In both cases the desire to have sex is driven by an underlying need. However, not all reasons or motivations for having sex are equal. We can divide these into two types of motivation for sex. For the sake of clarity we'll call these needs our 'golden motivations' and our 'shadow motivations'.

A golden motivation encompasses all the positive qualities we can apply to our desire to have sex. It stems from a place of empowerment, aliveness, abundance, joy, fun, playfulness, pleasure, connection, love, curiosity and so on. Its basis is self-confidence, self-love and self-expression. Importantly, a golden motivation is felt in the body as the life-force energy of our sexual self, which is longing for expression.

A shadow motivation is the opposite: here we have sex from a place of expectation, performance, need for power or fear of powerlessness, of rejection and abandonment. The driving force is ultimately loneliness, fear, lack of self-love and of self-confidence. A shadow motivation is not felt in the body as a natural urge for sexual self-expression, but stems from fear-based thoughts and emotional needs that make us stay in our head. Naturally, it is in these shadow motivations that we find most of the so-called sexual dysfunctions – the challenges that prevent the free expression of our innate sexual life-force energy.

Exercise: Motivations for Having Sex *(30 minutes)*

While the medical and much of the traditional therapeutic world is richly engaged in alleviating the perceived pathologies ranging from lack of libido to 'too much' libido, very little reflection is offered on understanding the deeper reasons for our 'normal' sexual behaviour. This exercise is designed to help you to understand all the subtle negotiations of emotional needs that are happening in your deeper psyche and that impact your sexual expression.

1. Start by making sure you have some quiet time to yourself, somewhere you won't be interrupted, and that your notebook and pen are close to hand.

2. Get in a comfortable position. Close your eyes and take a few moments to follow the natural flow of your breathing. Nothing else: just breathe consciously into your body and relax your mind.

3. Now, in your mind's eye, think of past sexual experiences you've had. Think about ones you've enjoyed, ones you recall as the best sex – and about the less satisfactory ones.

4. Think about each lover that you've had and what a typical sexual experience with them was like. Think, too, of any experiences of one-night stands or brief encounters.

5. Notice if there's a pattern. Do you tend to be the one to initiate sex or are you more passively receptive, waiting for the other to do it to you? How does this impact your experience?

6. Now begin to reflect on the deeper reasons why you had each kind of sexual experience. Do you have a tendency to have sex because you just want to feel alive or to enjoy pleasure? Or do you long to feel needed, special or important? Does having sex somehow give you an increased sense of self-worth, conquest or control? Was the motivation for sex on a one-night stand different from sex within a relationship?

7. Now see if you can find the golden and the shadow motivations for each kind of experience you've had. What compromises were you making? Were you able to be real or were you partly out of integrity? Write down a list of the different golden and shadow motivations that are particularly true for you.

8. Begin to notice how you feel about observing your patterns of behaviour. Do you feel empowered and happy, or sad and self-critical? The more aware you are, the more you can make conscious choices. It's through these acts of choice that you empower yourself. Whatever you observe, remember to be gentle with yourself.

THE ROAD MAP OF YOUR DESIRE

Having begun this reflection of why you are having sex, by looking at your golden and shadow motivations, it may be useful at this point to have a model that can help you to understand what's behind your unconscious driving forces. The following model arises from the psychotherapeutic modality known as Psychosynthesis, developed by the Italian psychiatrist and pioneer in transpersonal psychology, Roberto Assagioli.

When we look at any action we undertake, we can usually find there are different levels of meaning as to why we do what we do. Let's consider sex. At the first level of meaning there's the action itself: 'I have sex with someone.' We can call this the behaviour since it's the action we're performing.

However, this tells us nothing about what motivates us to have sex. When we examine this we need to ask ourselves, *Why do I want to have sex?* or *What do I want from the act of sex?* As we've seen from examining our golden and shadow motivations, there are many possible answers. One might be a desire for touch, another might be to feel closeness with another.

> **It's possible that we want to have sex because it gives us a feeling of having control over someone else.**

An example of this would be sex play where there's an exploration of a power exchange – think *Fifty Shades of Grey* (assuming this would be within the context of a healthy, consensual dynamic). We can label this level of our desire as our want: 'I "want" to have sex because...'.

Underneath the level of want there's a deeper level, a more profound motivation that ultimately acts as the driver for our actions. We can call this level of desire our need. We can uncover this by asking ourselves, if our desire to want was fulfilled, what deeper need would be satisfied?

Here's an example to illustrate the point. Imagine a woman who dutifully has sex with her husband because, she says, 'That's what's expected of me.' She may not enjoy it but feels it's her marital duty to 'give him what he wants' (probably a lesson learned in childhood, perhaps from observing her parents' relationship). So, at the level of behaviour, this woman is having sex with her husband; at the level of want we might say that she wants to meet her partner's desire for sex; at the deeper level of her need it might be that she has a need to feel that she has a sense of self-worth, or that by meeting her partner's desire for sex she makes herself secure in the relationship.

Once we understand the deeper level of desire, which we're calling our need, we can see the core quality of the behaviour. If we assume that the woman's need is to have a sense of self-worth – which she partly attains through giving her husband sex – then we could say that the core quality could be self-worth. Or if the need was to have a sense of security in the relationship, we could say that the core quality might be safety or security.

•••

When we examine any behaviour at this level of core quality, we can see that every action is intended to elicit a positive, valuable characteristic such as love, empowerment, safety, gratitude, grace, beauty, courage, self-worth, perseverance and resilience.

*Any core quality we find when we explore
at this level will be a positive quality.*

This is also true of our shadow motivations and the way they can be played out negatively. This might be hard to grasp in the first instance because sometimes shadow motivations appear to be thoughtless, negative or even malignant. It's true, of course, that some actions are harmful or unpleasant. This is because we distort the true core quality by failing to reflect on the impact on others or because we act regardless of consequences. However, if we can be patient enough to dig into our desires at this deep level, we can see that whatever our behaviour, it arises from a virtuous, positive core quality at its root.

When we apply this model of behaviour, wants and needs to the golden and shadow motivations, it becomes clear that behind every sexual encounter – behind every desired behaviour – there's a want and a need. Most importantly, however, behind every want and need there's a core quality that's always positive.

This can be very reassuring and helpful when we consider how we might sometimes be harsh on ourselves and judgmental for having certain types of desire, drive, fantasy or motivation for having sex. *I want to do this/have sex in this way/with this person – but that would be wrong*, we may tell ourselves. Or it might be that, in exploring our golden and shadow motivations, we realize that some of our desire for sex stems from a shadowy place of fear and insecurity within ourselves.

Although we might judge our desire as wrong or dirty at surface level, if we can reflect on it more deeply we can begin to see that this desire arises from a positive place within us.

Seen from this perspective, no drive or desire within us needs to be suppressed. No desire is, in itself, wrong; nor should it be judged and condemned. It just needs to find a way to express itself that is appropriate.

In very rare cases it may be that the actual act would be inappropriate if it were expressed – for example, if it were non-consensual. However, seeing that the impulse from which this arises is in itself positive, we can transform our energy around the desire so that we still get those deeper needs met. The question then becomes how to do this in ways that are appropriate.

WHAT IS HEALTHY SEX AND WHAT IS NOT?

As long as we view anyone else involved in our sexual behaviour as a human being similar to us, sharing our capacity for feelings and vulnerability, and with their own wants and needs; if we can maintain respect for others and for ourselves, we're having what we might describe as 'healthy' sex. It's important to understand this principle if you want to allow yourself to fully enjoy your sexuality.

When we hold a 'relational dynamic' – when we relate to the other as a human being, calling on the humanity within ourselves

– then any sexual activity we engage in is 'healthy', irrespective of what it might look like from the outside. This is why bondage and domination-submission play is 'healthy' as long as that fundamental aspect is in place.

> *Even if our desire is to be humiliated, punished*
> *or shamed, this is a 'healthy' desire if we respect*
> *ourselves as vulnerable human beings, as an 'I'.*

Similarly, desires to impose those experiences on others – to punish, humiliate, dominate – are equally 'healthy' if underneath the behavioural level of the activity we hold a respect for the other. We've already looked at how our culture can tend to objectify us but it is worth exploring further here the behavioural level of the activity we have respect for the other.

When sex is 'unhealthy' is when this relational dynamic is absent. This is most likely when one person seeks to fulfil their own desires without consideration of the other's feelings or condition. In the most extreme cases this looks like abuse, but on a lesser level it can be found in many conventional marriages and relationships where one party uses the other to get their needs met without considering their partner's feelings. At our clinic, female clients sometimes complain to us that it feels like their partner or spouse is 'masturbating inside them', while men can feel used if they get an erection when stimulated but aren't in the mood for sex. From this perspective even the simplest sexual act, when performed without this respect for the other, or for oneself, becomes 'unhealthy'.

> *Sex is less about 'what' we do and much*
> *more about 'how' and 'why' we do it.*

It can be very healing to remember this when we beat ourselves up for wanting sex with 'this' or 'that' person, or to have it in some way that we've been brought up to believe is not acceptable.

66

Exercise: Core Qualities and Unexpressed Desires
(45 minutes)

In this chapter we've been exploring how there are always underlying qualities – core qualities – that we're seeking to engage with when we connect with others for either sexual or emotional contact. This exercise is designed to help you discover the core qualities of your sexual expression and of the desires you might not yet have expressed. It builds on the previous exercise, 'Motivations for Having Sex' (see page 61), so you will need your notes from that exercise close to hand.

1. Make sure you have some undisturbed time for yourself, where you can be in a quiet, reflective state.

2. Take a few moments to relax your body and gently breathe into stillness. Feel yourself from a deeper place.

3. Go back to the list of motivations for having sex, where you realized your golden and shadow motivations. In this model they are the wants of your behaviour.

4. Go through the motivations (the wants) that you've listed, one by one. What was the underlying emotional need behind the sexual experiences? How did you want the experiences to make you feel? Give yourself some time to feel into it and write it down.

5. Now go a bit deeper into the enquiry. Behind the need there's a positive core quality. What core quality is that? If this need was met, how would you feel about yourself?

6. Take some time to reflect on this and write down your insights. What have you just learned about yourself? What positive core qualities are you longing to express in sex? How does it feel to realize that even behind shadow motivations there is a positive core quality?

7. Sit with this for a moment, breathe into your body and let the core qualities of your lovemaking become a part of your being.

8. Now write down a list of all the sexual activities you've fantasized about or would like to do but have never allowed yourself – maybe not even to fully acknowledge. Take your time.

9. Notice how you feel as you write down each desire. Do you feel excited or ashamed? Is it a mixture of both or something else? Notice if you want to edit out certain desires – and definitely include those ones.

10. Now examine each of the behaviours on this list and ask yourself, *What do I want from the sexual experience? What would I get from it and how would it make me feel different?*

11. Deepen the enquiry by feeling into the underlying need. Why do you have a desire to feel in this particular way? What deeper need would it meet?

12. Now feel into which core quality is expressed. Notice how even the desires you might hold a judgment towards always arise from a desire to experience yourself in a positive and expansive way and always point towards a desire for more love and connection.

13. End this exercise by taking some time to integrate these insights. Breathe into your body, realizing that all of this is you. Feel the love for yourself in this place.

WHAT IS THE NATURE OF DESIRE?

At the deepest level, desire responds to that most fundamental impulse – to seek connection. We see this as a two-stage process and we could include in this not only desire for sex but also any type of desire. When we consider the nature of desire, it helps to realize that we don't desire ourselves (much as we might narcissistically, or otherwise, love, admire and enjoy ourselves).

All desire is a felt sense of longing for that which is 'other' than us.

If we already have it, we cannot, by definition, desire it. We may enjoy it but we cannot desire it.

Desire arises from how we imagine we'll feel within ourselves when we meet the object of our desire, whether that is another person, an event or an experience. We might desire a glass of wine or a good meal because of the experience from our tongue or taste buds when we meet this other thing. We might long for contact with another person because of how we feel when we're with them. This understanding of desire also applies to emotional states. If we're feeling tired we might long to rest. If we feel stressed we may yearn for calmness. This is because we experience ourselves in relation to the otherness of that object or feeling.

It's only through the experience of contrast – that is to say, 'I feel like this' and 'You feel like that' – that we can experience ourselves. In other words, our desire for anything arises out of a desire for contact, with the person or object, and from a desire to feel the otherness of that contact. It's only through the experience of contrast that we can really 'feel' ourselves. If we're in contact with something that is exactly the same as ourselves, we don't experience it.

It's the space between us and the other that creates the desire, the longing to have contact with them or it.

This is the first stage of the process of desire, – the experience of self through contrast with the other.

Similarly, if we imagine two suns in the universe, we know that they are two suns because of the space that separates them. Now imagine that we can move those suns together so there's no space between them. How could we now tell where one sun ended and the other began? It's the space between the suns that gives them their uniqueness. It's the same with desire: it's the absence of the other – the space between us and the object or person of our desire – that creates the longing.

Once we merge with the otherness, as it's possible to do in profound lovemaking, we cease to experience ourselves as unique individuals and we become one with the other.

Our bodies move in rhythm, our breath synchronizes, our hearts seem to beat as one. If we're lucky enough and in tune enough to orgasm together, there may be a deep sense of melting into one another. This merging with the other is the second stage of desire.

So the nature of desire is at first to feel ourselves through the contrast with the otherness, followed by the felt otherness dissolving as we become one with the other. When eating a delicious meal or drinking wine we become one with it; in making love to the other, we merge with them.

This then begins to have a spiritual quality to it. Fundamentally, all spiritual traditions say that God (the divine, or whatever form the tradition believes to exist) created the universe in order to feel itself because by being at one with everything, the divine could not experience itself. The nature of the universe, say the spiritual traditions, is that it's constantly striving to know its true nature, which is its sense of oneness with all that is. This is the universal cycle, the rotation between separation and unity. We, too, long for the otherness in order to feel connection with it, to experience the return to oneness.

This is a very important point to be aware of in understanding your desire.

While sexual desire may ultimately be the longing to merge with the other, the desire is fuelled by the otherness, by what we're not yet merged with.

The core qualities of our lovemaking ultimately express a desire for love, unity and merging, while the separation is what keeps the desire alive. This is the polarity that makes the other attractive to us. This might help you to understand the dynamics of your desire: we're longing to merge with what we don't yet embody ourselves, so in this case our desires are our greatest gifts. If we listen to them and express them healthily and appropriately, they have the ability teach us our direction in life. When our desires are suppressed or denied we lose this very vital sense of direction, thus feeling dried out and empty, lacking meaning, purpose and direction.

Jane's Story

At 46, our client Jane had been married for over a decade. While she loved her husband, she just didn't enjoy sex with him and thought she had lost her libido. When asked what type of sex they were having, she described a sadly all-too-common experience. Her husband would briefly make amorous overtures towards her – perhaps a few moments of kissing or touching her breasts in bed – and then very quickly he would become aroused and move to penetration. After a few minutes he would climax, ejaculate, then hug her for a short while before turning over and going to sleep. Jane rarely had an orgasm, so unsurprisingly she had come to the conclusion that she did not enjoy sex. She was having sex with her husband out of duty, not out of pleasure.

When we explored the model of behaviours, wants and needs, Jane realized she was having sex because she was afraid her husband would abandon her. She had learned to take on the 'pleaser' part of herself to keep her husband happy. She was able to connect this to an experience in her childhood, of her father leaving her mother when she was only six years old.

Deep down, Jane had a fear of being abandoned, a shadow motivation that had held her in this unhealthy pattern of sexual behaviour for years.

When asked what she would like to be done differently, she responded, 'I'd like him to kiss me for longer. I'd like him to spend more time cuddling me and holding me. I want him to touch all of my body, to massage me, to stroke my back, to caress me and touch me gently like he used to. I want him to hold me for longer after we've finished having sex.'

It was obvious that Jane and her husband were limiting their understanding of what sex is to penetration. Jane thought that anything other than this wasn't sex, so her desires for other touch became nonsexual in her mind. This was significant in her belief that she no longer felt any desire for sex.

It was also clear that while her husband seemed satisfied with five minutes of penetrative sex, Jane had a much broader desire for sex than he did. Her own desires included kissing, cuddling, stroking, full-body touch and arousal, genital caressing, her own orgasmic pleasure as well as his. This insight was a turning point for her. It gave her confidence to understand she wasn't a woman who no longer wanted sex, but one who yearned for a more varied kind of sexual contact.

We worked with Jane on stepping out of her pleaser role and starting to communicate her needs and desires. Once she found her voice in asking for what she wanted, her husband and she began to explore different ways of lovemaking that more fully met her needs. This made her feel more alive in herself, and both her own and her husband's libido naturally increased accordingly.

Even though Jane's sexual behaviour had been driven by a shadow motivation of fear of abandonment, behind it she discovered the core quality of longing for love and safety. By making the change that was needed to take her marriage into a new and much more satisfying phase, she got exactly that without needing to compromise herself.

....

CONCLUSION

The first steps to having 'real sex' are to allow yourself to broaden your understanding of what constitutes sex and to understand that sex is not a goal-oriented pursuit but moves between sensual and sexual energies, evoking embodied presence with the other as well as life-force energy. You can also then begin to understand what drives your desire to have sex by looking at golden and shadow motivations and at the wants, needs and core qualities of your desire. Having an understanding of this information is going to help you to determine what kind of sex you want to have.

Looking at the list of deeper reasons why you want to have sex, you may find some of these needs are met and others are not. You may want to think about how you might be able to get those deeper needs met, in an appropriate way. For example, if a desire for loving connection is one of your core motivations for having sex, having wild, animalistic sex is unlikely to foster that desire for loving connection. On the other hand, if your desire is for wild abandon, then going softly with tender caresses is also unlikely to meet that need. Notice that there's no right or wrong way to have sex. It's simply about becoming aware of what your desires are and finding a way to allow them to be expressed.

Exercise: The Sexual Wheel of Life *(30 minutes)*

The Wheel of Life is a classical life-coaching tool, originally created by Paul J. Meyer to help you understand where in your life you are feeling fulfilled and where you might like to enhance your experience.[10] Here we've adapted it to help you get a new perspective on your sexual life. You'll need your notebook, a large piece of paper (ideally A3), a pen and colouring crayons.

I. Begin by making sure that you have some undisturbed time for yourself.

2. Draw a dot in the middle of the paper and 10 concentric circles around it, the biggest circle finishing at the edges of the paper, so that you've drawn something like a target.

3. Now, in your notebook, write down all the aspects of sex that are important to you. Take some time to really reflect on this and make sure you include what you've learned about yourself in the previous exercises. The aspects could be qualities like love, connection, wildness, playing with power, physical pleasure, fantasy, vulnerability, seduction, play, tenderness – to mention just a few. Feel into what is true for you.

4. Now reflect on each aspect. On a scale of 1–10, with 1 being the lowest fulfilment and 10 the highest, rate how much that desire is fulfilled right now.

5. When you've gone through the list, count the number of desires and divide your Wheel of Life into this number of same-size segments, as if you were cutting a circular cake.

6. Give each section the name of the desire and a colour, then colour in the area up to the rating you've given it, from the inside out, with 1 being the centre circle and 10 the outermost.

7. Take some time to reflect on your sexual Wheel of Life. How does it feel to have a visual overview of your desires and the amount to which they are fulfilled? Where would you like to expand?

KEY 2:
KNOW YOUR SEXUAL SELF

If you've explored the exercises in the last chapter, we hope you're beginning to have a sense of what it is you want your sexual life to look like and what desires you have at this moment. It's worth doing these exercises more than once because each time you do them and become more comfortable with the process, you are likely to reach deeper levels of what you wish for sexually and be better able to healthily integrate your sexuality into your life. Remember that whatever comes out of the exercises is not negative, even if you feel blocked or if desires and impulses arise about which you might be judgmental. Every desire has at its centre a positive core quality. Now, having looked at 'what' you wish for in your sexual life, we need to consider the next question: 'who' is it that wants this?

So far, the road map of your desire contains your behaviours, your wants, your needs and the core quality at the heart of your behaviours. We can complete this picture by adding another layer of meaning to this model and saying that each of these behaviours comes from a different part of you.

It's easy to have the illusion that 'you' consists of one, fixed persona. We might feel we're defined by our job, our role as a spouse or parent, by the colour of our skin, by our religion or gender, and we might believe that we have a fixed way of behaving according to this identity. But if we look at this more closely, it's not true: we behave in different ways in different scenarios. Take the way you behave at work – it's probably quite different from the way you behave with friends or a lover.

For example, as sex therapists we have developed Psychosexual Somatics®. Using our professional skills in this area is essential for our work. However, if we started analysing our friends and their relationships, we would soon run out of friends. So we behave differently depending on whether we're with friends or clients.

We all know that we'll react differently to the same situation at different times. Sometimes you might go to a party feeling confident, effervescent and outgoing; at other times you might be shy and retiring. This wouldn't happen if you were always the same person, with a fixed personality.

> *Each of us has multiple aspects to our personality that come into play, and operate very differently, at different times.*

Let's call these aspects 'mini-characters'. The mini-characters are more than just moods. They are entire personalities with their own beliefs, agendas, associated emotions and entire complex views of the world. They also have their own needs that often compete with other mini-characters within us. It can be helpful to give these mini-characters names to help identify and relate to them more easily.

Having a wide range of mini-characters within us in no way suggests that we're all suffering from split personalities or that there's something wrong with us. Having different aspects of ourselves allows each of us to vary our responses to situations, and to create the richness and depth of personality that gives us deep and meaningful relationships and sexual experiences.

> *The more mini-characters we're in touch with, the more developed our personality and our ability to have good sex.*

As an example, let's look at a mini-character that will be familiar to most readers: one that takes a self-critical part. That part might sit waiting for you not to be 'perfect' or for you to 'get it wrong' and then they pounce: 'You didn't do that very well, did you?' we might hear a voice in our head saying. We could call this part, simply, the Critic. In most people, the Critic isn't always present, but it may be activated by certain situations. It often shows up most frequently in relationships. Perhaps it kicks in when we find our partner withdrawing or not meeting our needs. Perhaps the Critic becomes active when we don't perform in the way we expect ourselves to in the bedroom. There may be a tendency to judge ourselves harshly and to assume the blame, no matter what the reality is.

Our external reality is a projection of our internal landscape, and if you strongly identify with one particular mini-character you will tend to see the world filtered through their lens, rather than as an objective reality.

> *In effect, mini-characters create an*
> *altered perception of reality.*

Some distorted beliefs we might hold, perhaps as a result of watching pornography or reading women's fashion magazines, might include, 'Everyone has orgasms, so if I can't, there must be something wrong with me', or 'I should be able to make my partner orgasm, otherwise I must be no good at sex.' If we believe these viewpoints and find ourselves lacking, we might, instead of enjoying sex and intimacy, choose to avoid relationships or sexual experiences because they make us feel inadequate. Such feelings of inadequacy are not real. They are a product of overidentifying with a certain mini-character and believing the stories it tells us.

> *Where these mini-characters are linked*
> *to strong feelings of vulnerability, their*
> *foundation often dates back to childhood.*

It can be surprising how frequently these childhood vulnerabilities continue to rule our lives and govern how we have sex and relationships – in a very unhealthy way.

None of these mini-characters is innately good or bad. As we discussed in the previous chapter, we're subject to behaviours that have underneath them wants, needs and core qualities. As well as having these aspects, every mini-character has both a gift and a limitation. The Critic makes a good example. At first glance this may appear to be an unhelpful or negative aspect of us. However, if we didn't have a part of us that was critical, we would soon become arrogant and self-important.

So rather than dismiss the Critic, we just need to keep that part in balance. The limitation of the Critic may be that it stops us from expressing ourselves fully; the gift may be that it prevents us from being narcissistic or perhaps from becoming lazy.

Remember, too, that if you watch pornography, the actors are also playing mini-characters. Just like stars in a normal movie, how they behave on film is not who they are as actors. They're simply playing a role, informed by one mini-character or another within them, and it can be entertaining when watching pornography to see which mini-character is being played on screen – the Seductress, the Innocent, the Stud, the Submissive and so on.

One of the most fruitful ways we can utilize this idea of mini-characters is in sex.

The joy of having multiple 'mini-characters'
is that they allow us to have more varied and
more interesting sexual experiences.

If we believe that the only way we can have sex is by being tender, loving, slow and gentle, then while this might be beautiful in some circumstances, it might also stop us from expressing other desires or impulses that would be inconsistent with that role. There might be another part of us that wants to have wild and abandoned sex, or a part that enjoys being seductive, or the act and art of being seduced. Perhaps sometimes we have a desire to make love and sometimes to have sex. One day we may feel like being more dominant; on another day we might wish to explore our submissiveness. It can be fun to give these different parts names: the Seductress, the Femme Fatale, the Gigolo, the Shy Boy/Girl, the Virgin, the Sensitive Lover, the Wild Man/Woman and so on. It's less fun, of course, if the mini-character is the Dutiful Spouse.

Remember when you watch pornography that the actors are almost always, by definition, in the mini-character of the Performer. This mini-character needs to perform in order for the movie to be made. It needs to demonstrate desire for sex and have a willingness to engage in anything required of it (the latter usually applies to a female). If the Performer is male, he'll often be required to ejaculate. Such demonstrations are not reality. They are simply mini-characters that the actors play or identify with in order to do their job. This does not mean that all porn stars are constantly having sex when off the set. Remember not to believe pornography.

Too often it's easy to compare ourselves to pornography and believe that we need to be in the Performer in sex. Like all mini-characters, there's nothing wrong with the Performer – sometimes. However, if you believe that this is how you 'have' to be in order to have good sex, you will soon find yourself trapped in ideas about performance, caught up in thoughts about whether you're 'good enough' and having a very one-dimensional experience of sex – both with yourself and with your sexual partner or partners.

If you limit yourself to making love as one 'mini-character', your sexual experiences will be limited and soon become boring.

Variety keeps us alive and is one of the best ways of ensuring a long and satisfying sexual life. This doesn't mean that we need necessarily have a variety of partners. It means that we need to access different parts of our self and have sex or make love from those different parts in order to continue feeling desire and aliveness in a relationship. By bringing forwards a different mini-character within yourself, you are also giving your partner an opportunity to introduce a new part of themselves and a different experience of sexual intimacy. Consequently, when you access different mini-characters, you are in effect having sex with someone different each time without needing to break the agreements if you are in a monogamous relationship.

Exercise: Sexual Self Mini-Character *(30 minutes)*

Having understood the idea of mini-characters, we can begin to explore some of these sexual parts of your self. We'll work with a visualization, and even if this is new to you, be reassured there is no 'wrong' way to do this. If images don't come to you easily, just imagine how the scenario would feel. Use your senses and trust that whatever comes into your imagination is what you need at this moment, even if your mind does not make sense of it.

1. Make sure that you are sitting or lying comfortably, with your notebook and pen to hand, and that you won't be disturbed. Close your eyes and bring your awareness inside. Take a few minutes to drop deeply into your body and to relax.

2. Imagine that you are in a meadow – the most beautiful, wonderful meadow you've ever seen. Use your senses to feel the sun on your skin, the grass under your feet. Notice the scent of the grass and the flowers, the sound of birds.

3. As you look up, you notice a little forest in the distance. You feel a strong urge to move towards that forest, so you start walking towards it, feeling a sense of excitement as you're approaching.

4. As you reach the forest, you see a little path leading you into the woods. Sense the change in atmosphere as you walk into the trees. Feel the excitement building as you notice a clearing among them.

5. As you enter the clearing, look around and pause for a moment. Feel the beauty of this place. Enjoy the quiet stillness.

6. But wait! There's some movement in the trees. With excitement you realize that this is your Sexual-self-as-it-is-now mini-character, which has decided to show itself to you; who you are sexually at this point of your life.

7. Allow this part of you to appear out of the woods. It might be a person or an animal, or even an object. It might not make sense to you. Just trust that this image is what you need to see. Who, or what, are you sexually?

8. Get a really good look at this being. Notice how you feel towards it. Notice how your body responds to its presence. Is your impulse to approach it or to back away from it?

9. Your Sexual-self-as-it-is-now wants to tell you something. What is it saying? What are its desires? What does it want and need? What are its fears and limitations? What are its core qualities? Give yourself plenty of time to listen.

10. Is there anything you'd like to say in response? Take your time to feel into it.

11. When it feels complete for you, thank this part for having shown itself to you, slowly turn around and begin to walk back through the clearing, along the path through the forest and back into the meadow.

12. When you are back in the meadow, pause for a moment. Thank yourself for having the courage to take this journey and to return with the gifts you received.

13. In your own time, when you feel ready, gently open your eyes and come back into the room.

14. Write down some notes about the qualities and gifts that this exercise revealed to you.

WHAT WE SUPPRESS

Hopefully, in the last exercise you were able to get in touch with a part of your sexuality that you know well and with which you feel most comfortable. But what else is there in your sexuality? Which parts of your sexual self do you not express, and why not?

Our sexual energy is also commonly called erotic energy. Let us consider this term for a moment. The word 'erotic' derives from the Greek god Eros. Eros was the god of love, but of a specific kind of love: Eros celebrated the love of life.

The word 'erotic' has become sexual but its
true meaning is far broader than this.

To the ancient Greeks, Eros was wild, passionate, fiery and fierce. Since the term 'erotic' now has too many modern cultural limitations, we'll refer to the truer meaning of the word by calling it 'Eros energy'. Eros energy is the raw power of the life force itself.

When we allow our bodies to dance without limitation, when we roar with joy at a sporting victory, when we throw ourselves into any physical activity with our totality, this is Eros energy. When we're total in our lovemaking, this is Eros energy. Eros energy gives rise to pleasure.

When we feel pleasure we feel it in our bodies. It's this Eros energy that we're feeling, whether it's sexual pleasure or simply the pleasure of some delicious food or the pleasure of having done some really good exercise. These pleasures are of the body – they are felt in the body and they are pleasures of the senses, which we may experience as sensual or sexual, depending on the nature of the experience and the context. For example, having a hug from one person might be a sensual pleasure; receiving the same hug from another person might feel far more sexual.

However, pleasure and the accompanying Eros energy can feel dangerous. They may feel uncontrolled or unpredictable. Eros, for the ancient Greeks, represented a quality to be embraced cautiously, mindful that it could get out of control; the raw potency of uncontained Eros energy could be disruptive and destructive. It became important, then, to contain and control this energy, to ensure that stability and order are maintained in society. Too much Eros energy and too much pleasure could mean that people don't go to work, they don't honour their relationships, they become selfishly focused on their personal, hedonistic pleasure without thought of others and one another's boundaries. So the pleasure principle and this Eros energy were suppressed.

This is one of the primary functions of civilization as it has developed: to cut us off from our primal, instinctive behaviours.

> ***If we surrendered to our Eros energy, we would no longer be useful, functional members of society.***

We would become self-indulgent and uncontrolled in our emotions. Our primal feelings might emerge in too raw a form, whether that is desire or rage.

As explained in the Introduction, it's these twin energies of sex and anger that have been outsourced in our culture. Sex, or desire, is projected onto objects we want (so often sold with sexual imagery), which makes them, in effect, a fetish. ('If only I had that new thing, I'd be happy.') Anger, meanwhile, is projected onto 'the dangerous other', such as al-Qaida or so-called Islamic State.

By being displaced, our primal urges are made safe to others within our culture. However, this displacement comes at enormous cost. We become disconnected from our bodies and we unconsciously disown our sexual drives, allowing ourselves to be satisfied with the scraps of desire we feel are permitted.

The greatest enforcer of this displacement is shame. Shame arises because we have an internal impulse to do something, but external rules – morality – tell us that it's not allowed.

> ***Shame is what stops us from accessing our Eros energy.***

Shame is what inhibits our ability to express ourselves fully. Shame keeps us locked into cycles of fear.

Take the simple example of dancing. For most of us, it takes a couple of drinks to get us out onto the dance floor. Even then, we move our bodies in limited ways, restricting our body's expression so that we don't cause ourselves to feel embarrassed. We don't take the risk of expressing ourselves freely because we fear shame.

It's even more the case in sex. Too often we tell ourselves that we couldn't express 'that' desire because it wouldn't be understood; it wouldn't be acceptable; we would be rejected – and we would feel shame for having had the desire in the first place. Our culture so deeply suppresses free sexual expression that by the time we're adults we've naturally internalized this and barely need anyone to judge us. We simply do it ourselves.

Exercise: Where Is Shame in Your Body? *(20 minutes)*

Since we experience shame in the body and since it's an uncomfortable feeling, it makes sense that we might try to avoid it. The only way to avoid shame when it's present in our body is to disconnect from our body; to cut ourselves off from it. Try this experiment to see where you carry shame in your body.

1. Stand up with your feet about shoulder-width apart. Close your eyes and bring your awareness into your body. Take some nice deep breaths and feel your feet on the ground. Notice how it feels, just standing there.

2. Now take a moment to recall something in your life that caused you feelings of shame. We suggest that the first time you do this exercise you choose something minor. Perhaps it was something embarrassing that you said as a child, perhaps you acted in a way that you later regretted – perhaps under the influence of alcohol or maybe drugs.

3. Focus your attention on the memory of that mildly shameful incident. If at any point it feels too much, you can come out of the exercise by opening your eyes and reminding yourself that you are safe and simply recalling a memory.

4. Notice what you feel. And notice where you feel it in your body. Does your body feel open and spacious or does it want to contract and maybe curl up?

5. Now allow your body to take on the shape that it wants to as you connect with those feelings of shame. You might find your body wants to curl into a ball, to put your hands over your face and hide from the world. You may discover that you feel like making yourself as small as possible. Whatever shape your body wants to take, allow that to happen.

6. As you move into the body position, notice where the most tense, contracted or frozen parts of your body are. Is there a focal point of the contraction or twisting? Once you can locate that, you have a sense of where your body is holding shame.

7. Now breathe into that place and gently stretch it into an opposite body posture, stretching or massaging the contracted or frozen part of your body so that it opens up. Bring your awareness to your body and notice any emotions, sensations or judgments that come up and how the feeling of shame changes.

8. We are not suggesting that simply stretching will cure you of shame. However, when you consciously become aware of how you are storing shame in your body and stay present with it, you can create space between yourself and the shame. You are observing it instead of believing it. Once you've moved through the discomfort and into an open body posture, you'll be able to be present with your pleasure.

9. We suggest that you try this exercise three times in a row, each time seeing if you can allow yourself to go deeper into the felt experience of shame in your body before releasing it.

10. Be gentle with yourself as you come out of this exercise; you may have got in touch with some powerful and uncomfortable feelings. Do not push yourself too hard. Allow your body to guide you into the level it knows it can work with at present.

MINI-CHARACTERS THAT STOP US FROM FEELING PLEASURE

In effect, we develop mini-characters who don't allow themselves (that is, us) pleasure or allow free reign of our sexual desires. We manage to tell ourselves that we don't really desire this or that, that we wouldn't enjoy it even if we could have it and that if we did have it, it wouldn't be okay – for us, for our partner, for our parents, for our friends, for society at large. Think about people coming out as gay and the struggle many of them have because their desires weren't historically seen as healthy, acceptable, moral or legal – depending on which period in history we're talking about. Whatever sexual orientation we self-identify as, we all have sexual desires that we believe are not okay, which limit us from expressing ourselves as free and full sexual beings.

By examining those parts of ourselves where we have internal judgments, such as 'I'm not allowed to do that,' 'No one will want me,' or 'That's disgusting,' we can begin to understand how we limit our sexual pleasure and how to restore it to its rightful place in our lives.

It's worth noting that it's what we absolutely don't want to look at that contains the greatest gold.

FROM FANTASY TO REALITY

One place that such limitations are often least felt is in our fantasies. Since fantasies are something that we can choose to keep private, we may give ourselves more freedom here than in the parts of our sexuality that are externally expressed. Perhaps you have a fantasy of being submissive, of being forced into sex. Perhaps you fantasize about people you know you can't have sex with in real life or about having more than one lover at a time.

The most important thing to say about fantasies is that they are never 'wrong'. Some fantasies may be wonderful to act out; others may be best left to the imagination. Whatever the fantasy, don't judge yourself for it.

> *Remember that underneath each desire is a*
> *deeper meaning, a* core quality *that is beautiful –*
> *whatever we may feel about the fantasy itself.*

The fastest way to make something erotically charged is to make it unavailable or taboo. This is why 'the grass is always greener': we always want what we cannot have, and whatever isn't allowed is even more exciting. Having fantasies about people or situations that we don't give ourselves permission to truly feel is a certain way to create erotic energy about it.

John's Story

John, a gentle and slightly shy guy of 35, came to our practice because he felt ashamed of his sexuality. He was secretly watching porn every day, becoming attracted to more and more intense scenarios, and his sexual fantasies featured practices he himself judged as 'extreme' and 'dirty'. Sex with his girlfriend was challenging because he felt he was having sex with her as an obligation and needed to go into fantasy to get really aroused and able to reach orgasm.

He was ashamed of his desires and felt isolated as he wasn't able to tell his girlfriend or anyone else about his real turn-ons.

> *He was also self-judgmental that something was*
> *'wrong' with him because he had these fantasies.*

By exploring the fantasies together, it became clear that he felt a strong charge around submission, humiliation and being taken to his limits, where he had no choice but to surrender. In terms of the behaviour (as we described earlier in this chapter), the sexual practices of his fantasies were about being overpowered in a way that most people would experience as physically uncomfortable.

As we started digging deeper, his want was to be taken and dominated; to be 'done to' so that he would feel completely powerless, which was the need that was driving his desires. By observing his need for powerlessness, he was able to access the underlying core quality, which in this case was to surrender to the feminine.

This need to surrender was a deep longing in him that he found extremely hard to deal with in real life. He realized he was holding a resentment towards women that made him close down even though he was longing to feel connection. As we explored his relationship with his mother, it emerged that as a baby he hadn't received the nurture and care that he needed and had become disconnected from the needs and sensations of his body. He had experienced his mother as smothering and controlling, and as a healthy defence to keep his masculine core safe he had developed an inner resistance to women. While he was longing to surrender, he also distrusted women and would not let them in. He would live out his desire to surrender in the safety of his fantasies, where he would inhabit a mini-character who was dependent and surrendered, and safe enough to feel his body and become aroused.

Once John had explored the core quality that lay beneath his desires, he began to understand that they weren't shameful. He had hidden and suppressed his Eros energy because he felt his masculine core was unsafe with women. This had created a power game and a taboo in himself that was charged with all the erotic power he had stored away.

John understood that he was playing out his resentment towards women in his relationships and by withholding his sexuality, which ultimately led him to feelings of shame and isolation. This understanding helped him allow himself more vulnerability, to come into deeper connection with his girlfriend, to feel more and to discharge bit by bit the energy that kept him fixated on these fantasies. He could now focus on a wider range of sexual excitement without it needing to be triggered by his taboo fantasies. As he was now in a position of choice about his sexual expression, the urgency and shame subsided and he was able to enjoy his fantasies as an addition to his living, connected sexuality.

. . . .

Exercise: Exploring Fantasy *(30 minutes)*

As John's case demonstrates, some people feel shame about their fantasies and allow them or act them out only in isolation, either on their own in private or with one other person, not allowing this part of themselves be seen more widely. Other people enjoy them freely on their own or with like-minded partners, while some people (with a majority of women in this group) claim they have no sexual fantasies. Either way, this exercise is designed to deepen your self-awareness about the edges of your inner erotic life: your fantasies.

1. You'll need a notebook and pen for this exercise, and a quiet and undisturbed space in which to reflect.

2. Start by reflecting on the following questions: Do you ever fantasize? How do you feel about fantasizing or not fantasizing? Do you fantasize on your own or with a partner? If on your own, does your partner know? How do you feel about that? Are your fantasies more like glimpses of random daydreams about people you know or feel attracted to, or are they more detailed scenarios, about things you might or might not even want to experience in real life?

3. Write a few notes about what you're learning so far.

4. Put your notebook and pen aside and make sure you're comfortable and relaxed in your body, either sitting or lying.

5. Close your eyes and breathe into your body with deep, slow breaths, as you turn your awareness inwards, preparing to awaken your desire.

6. Keep breathing, and notice how even just intending desire may be enough to awaken a slight stirring in your body.

7. Now tune in to one of your fantasies that your mind might have a slight judgment about, or something you would like to do sexually but might not have had the courage or opportunity to experience.

8. Breathe slowly, sensually into your body as you're doing that. Allow your body to respond and to open up to the scenario that you're imagining.

9. If you feel unable to fantasize and cannot think of something you would like to experience, think of the way you usually have sex and imagine what the exact opposite behaviour would look like. Imagine how this not-you person would have sex, and slowly, sensually breathe into your body. Notice if your body is somehow open to the possibility of expressing itself sexually in a different way. If feelings of self-judgment come up, gently put them aside and come back into the experience in the body.

10. Now tune in to the part of you that is having this experience. If your fantasy was a theatre play, which character were you playing? Who is the mini-character in action? What do they look like? How do they behave?

11. How are you, the observer, feeling about the behaviour of this mini-character?

12. Behind this behaviour, can you start feeling into the want, the need and the core quality? What is the message, at the deepest sense, to you from this mini-character? What qualities does it bring?

13. Having understood the core quality, come back to your physical, bodily experience. Does this understanding change anything for you in the way you allow yourself to enjoy the fantasy?

14. Feel the 'Yes' in your body, allowing the core qualities of this mini-character. Breathe into it and enjoy!

15. End the exercise by writing some notes about what you have learned about yourself.

For John, part of his fear was that if his desire was fully expressed, it would be seen as 'too much'. When we have these feelings that the other will judge us for our desires, it's easy to edit them out of our lives or even out of our awareness. By doing so we keep ourselves small, we don't inhabit our sexual self as fully as we might and we deny not only our own pleasure but also the potential for pleasure in our partner.

However, very often when one person has a desire, the other will also have a similar desire if they can give themselves permission to express it. In fact, when we deny ourselves and do not show a part of ourselves to our partner, we deny them the opportunity to love that part of us. The more you show of yourself, the more of yourself you make available to be loved.

> *When we limit our desires through fear of judgment, we also give the implicit message to our partner that their desire is not okay, either.*

When we show those parts of us, we give them permission to express themselves more fully, too.

WHEN WE EDIT OURSELVES

Stifling our desires is one of the fundamental reasons why in most normal relationships sex eventually becomes routine and unfulfilling. At the start of a sexual relationship you probably try out your best moves; you are typically more open to exploring desire with one another. It may be that the hormones involved in that feeling of being 'in love' override our internal judgments.

However, as we explore our sexual identity with our new partner, over time we find that a part of us is not met, not seen or accepted. In short, we learn that some of our desires are not okay. It may be that one night we tried something and our partner wasn't in the mood for it. It may be that we unknowingly stumbled upon some secret fear or judgment in them. Whatever it is, we tell ourselves, 'That wasn't okay,' and make a mental note of what they didn't like.

So we edit ourselves. We begin not to show those parts we feel are, or might be, judged, and gradually we find that we're restricted to a limited expression of self, both sexually and in other ways. Our sexual interaction becomes less and less creative. Partly we feel that we know what works – *I know he/she likes this and this and this. I know that if I do those things he/she will have an orgasm*. It can begin to feel like getting the job done rather than a mutual exploration of pleasure and connection.

> **Partly we edit our sexual expression with the other so that we bring only what is safe and we know won't be rejected.**

When we begin to do this, we begin effectively to put a stop not only to our sexual growth but also to our personal growth.

> **In fact, the type of sex we have is limited by how far we've developed our sense of self.**

Think of it this way. Imagine that you find your genitals embarrassing and dirty. If this were true you might not enjoy oral sex, where your genitals are 'up close and personal' to your partner. If you develop psychologically to the point where you can accept and love your genitals, you will be able to enjoy oral sex. But perhaps you still think that your bottom is 'dirty'. Any kind of anal pleasure would therefore be unthinkable. In order to enjoy this you need to come to love your bottom and give yourself permission to experience pleasure in that area.

So when we hit resistances to sexual pleasure, it's important to look at whether we're limiting ourselves because we've not explored our relationship with a particular body part or a sexual activity. When doing this, you can look at what beliefs might be activated by a certain type of sex. Which mini-characters are holding those beliefs? Perhaps this part of you feels younger than you are – a teen, a child or even an infant. How old does that part of you feel, and where do those ideas that this sexual act is wrong, perhaps dirty or shameful, come from?

If we can explore our own sexual limitations, and understand where they come from and how they might hold us back, rather than just rush to make a judgment by saying, 'That's just wrong,' then we give ourselves – and those around us, including our partners – the opportunity to grow and develop. So when we find something difficult or uncomfortable in ourselves, we won't be judgmental about that part when we see it in others. What's more, if we cannot own and accept this in ourselves, we tend to imagine that others have this part (whether we see that as good or bad) and when we do that, which we call projecting, we give away our power because we see those qualities in others rather than in ourselves.

> *The path to sexual empowerment is to stop projecting our sexuality onto others and begin to make friends with it, to integrate it more fully into our own lives.*

We can do this by exploring which parts or mini-characters of our sexuality we deny or suppress and which parts we allow. The more sexual mini-characters we have, the more integrated we become as a whole person. Remember, even those mini-characters we judge unfavourably will have at their centre a core quality that is beautiful and empowering and that does us good to get in touch with. The more we recognize our limitations, the more we recognize our strengths.

> *The more we show of ourselves, the more we make available to be loved.*

Exercise: What Do You Deny in Your Sexuality?
(20 minutes)

There are many reasons why we inhibit our sexual expression, but fear of judgment is a major one. This exercise will give you a sense of how to integrate aspects of your sexuality that you might see in others but deny in yourself.

1. Have your notebook and pen close to hand, and make sure you have some undisturbed time on your own.

2. Take a few moments to connect with yourself: close your eyes and breathe into your body.

3. Now think of a person who you consider to be really sexy and sexually confident. It might be a celebrity or someone known to you personally.

4. Let the image become really clear in your mind. Notice how they dress, how they move their body, their facial expressions.

5. Now begin to notice how you feel as you watch them. Do you feel excited, happy, jealous, insecure, judgmental or something else?

6. Notice how your body feels as you observe them. Do you feel expansion or contraction in your body when watching them? What else do you notice in your body?

7. Move your awareness closer and closer to the person. Imagine you can slip into their skin and become that person. It doesn't matter if they are the same gender or the opposite – just play with the idea of becoming them and really feel what it's like.

8. Now get up and begin to move about the room as though you are that person. Maybe you want to dance, maybe you want to move your pelvis. Just follow the impulses in your body.

9. Allow your movements to become increasingly sexual and notice how that feels. What qualities do you get in touch with when you pretend to be this other person?

10. Once you really have a feel for this person, let go of the role-play and come back to yourself. Stand still on the floor. Close your eyes again if you've opened them and notice how you feel in your body. Do you feel differently than you normally do?

11. Gently open your eyes, sit back down and make some notes about your experience. What did you discover? Were there any new energies within you that you got in touch with?

Now you've done the exercise, let us share the secret behind it: whatever you got in touch with is nothing but a part of you. Whatever we imagine about other people is just a projection of unowned parts of ourselves. It wasn't the person you were thinking of who expressed what you just felt or moved or danced – but you. It was you giving yourself permission. By using the other as an 'excuse', we can access parts of ourselves that we might have a judgment about and have therefore normally shut off.

The next time you have sex or make love, you might like either to imagine that you are playacting the person you thought about or to get in touch with the qualities you felt in yourself when you role-played them. Perhaps a new part of your sexual self is emerging that wants to play and enjoy itself. Give yourself permission to explore that and to enjoy it.

SEX STARTS WITH YOU

Hopefully the previous exercise has shown you that the qualities of sexuality that you were previously projecting onto other people are actually something you can access within yourself.

This is an important point. Our culture has a very distorted view of sexuality. It seems to be telling us that sex is something that happens when we meet someone else. If we believe this to be true then we become dependent on others to make us feel sexual. It's like the princess waiting for her prince to come. She waits helplessly and in doing so loses her power, making herself reliant on someone else's actions.

This happens a lot in sex. It seems that women, especially, enter a story where they cannot be sexual unless someone else does something to them. For some it's about not allowing their sexuality without someone else turning them on. For others it's a case of waiting for someone to 'give them' an orgasm.

> *The idea that we need someone else to make us feel sexual is a guaranteed way to give up our sexual power.*

But really we don't need anyone else to wake up our sexuality. It's something that is within each of us and that we can awaken within ourselves. Yes, it can be delicious to share that energy with others, but it's not a prerequisite for us to feel it.

> *The more we explore our sexual selves with ourselves, the better we get to know it and the more comfortable we become with it.*

When we allow ourselves to explore the variety and variations of our sexual self-expression, we can really learn what turns us on and the range of possibilities this can offer for us to feel sexually alive.

SELF-PLEASURE!

We've already started to look at how we can reframe our relationship with fantasy by examining its deeper meaning and by giving ourselves permission to allow our desires. We can now begin to expand this into an essential practice when learning to love your sexuality: self-pleasuring.

The term self-pleasuring has none of the negative connotations that 'masturbation' has for many people. Self-pleasuring is also a more self-loving term and hopefully a more accurate one. Since sexuality begins with oneself, exploring our own body's pleasure is a key part of this.

> ### *How can you ask someone else to give you sexual pleasure if you don't know yourself what feels good?*

Through a regular practice of self-pleasuring you will gain many benefits. Firstly you will understand how your body can give you pleasure. You'll also come to love your sexuality more fully and become more comfortable with it.

> ### *Self-pleasuring is an act of self-empowerment. When you can give yourself pleasure, you no longer become reliant on others to do it for you.*

You'll better learn the subtle nuances of your body's response, and through taking responsibility for your pleasure and your desire you'll take back some of the sexual potency you may have given to others. In addition, the more that you self-pleasure and get to know your sexual self, the clearer you can become about your boundaries. Once you know what you enjoy and what you don't, you will be more able to communicate those boundaries to others.

You can continue your journey to more fully knowing your sexual self by taking up a daily practice of self-pleasuring for at least 30 days. Perhaps you already self-pleasure regularly; perhaps this will be the first time you try something like this. In either case, we invite you to make this a new experience. Since sexual energy is focused on the genitals, it's easy to make them the centre of self-pleasuring. However, for this exercise, and as a general guideline for having more 'real sex', we recommend that you start not with touching your genitals but with engaging your whole body in arousal. It's not only your genitals that are an 'erogenous zone' but your whole body. Every inch of your body can give you pleasure, so why limit it to the genitals?

Exercise: Self-Pleasuring in a New Way (at least 60 minutes)

Whether you self-pleasure regularly or not, we suggest imagining that you've never done this before and that you are simply exploring your body with curiosity, trying to learn what feels good for you. What you are looking for is reconnection with the richness of sensations and the subtle pleasures that are innate in the body. With every movement, consciously go slowly, feel, become aware of sensation and emotions that may be present, and breathe.

1. Start by making sure you have privacy and quiet time, and create a warm and nurturing space for your senses to enjoy. This might be turning down the light, burning some aromatic oils, lighting some candles or playing some sensual music. You can also start by taking a warm bath with sensual oils. Whatever brings you into your body and helps you to relax fully.

2. You may choose to do this exercise sitting or lying down on a bed or the floor. The most important thing is to be comfortable.

3. Take some time to relax and breathe into your body, just feeling yourself in this moment.

4. When you're ready, start slowly exploring your body, perhaps touching your neck, face, cheeks, the sides of your hands and arms. Stroke or caress your body slowly and lovingly, and enjoy the sensations of it.

5. You can add some props to help vary the sensation – pieces of fur, silk, ostrich or similar feathers, even cold metal or a warm (though not hot) cup of tea on the skin can all feel delicious.

6. Explore which different sensations give you pleasure. Your touch can be soft and slow or scratchy and stimulating. Notice how your body responds to different kinds of touch, and give yourself what you enjoy in each moment. Take your time.

7. Once you've woken up your whole body, you can begin to include more directly erogenous areas in your touch, like the inner thighs, lips, breasts and nipples. Try different types of touch in those areas – light, firm, pinching, squeezing, stroking, gently brushing and so on.

8. Allow your body to move and your hips, belly and spine to undulate with the energy of pleasure you're accumulating in your body.

9. Make sounds! Breathe, sigh, groan! Let your voice help the sensations vibrate physically through your body.

10. Once your body feels alive you can gently begin to include your genitals. Include them in your touch as you would any other part but don't ignore the rest of your body. Go really slowly, as if you had never felt your genitals before.

11. When the energy starts to build and you want to focus more on the genitals, don't do so with the intention of trying to have an orgasm. Simply let your body guide you towards its pleasure.

12. If you become highly aroused and orgasmic that is absolutely fine but don't make it the goal of this exercise.

13. Make sure to pause regularly, breathe and feel the whole of your body. Where is the pleasure? Which sensations do you notice that you are usually unaware of?

14. When the exercise feels complete for you, make some notes about what you learned about yourself.

When you learn to allow yourself to experience different types of pleasure in your body in different ways, you are well on the way to learning more about your sexual self, which is a key part of the journey towards 'real sex'. You might be able to use this information to play with different mini-characters and ways of expressing yourself sexually, which can create a new sense of ownership of your sexuality.

When you have different ranges of expression, you are in a position of choice about how to express yourself; you're not doomed to repeat the well-trodden patterns that might feel safe but will end up boring and limiting.

Every time you risk an expression slightly
out of your comfort zone, you grow.

Even though you might feel challenged by inner judgments about certain ways of expressing yourself, every behaviour has at its root a core quality that is always positive.

Applying this perspective to your fantasies and unexpressed desires can be hugely helpful in removing the shame we've been taught to feel about aspects of our natural Eros energy that don't fit within the norms of 'civilized' society. What's more, by owning that part of your sexual self, you are adding to a freer and more real way of being that doesn't involve relying on others to make you feel a certain way. Remember, sex starts with you, and the more you know about your own pleasures, turn-ons and desires, the more you will be able to create fulfilling experiences for yourself and for those with whom you share yourself.

KEY 3:
RECLAIM YOUR BODY

The disconnection from the Eros energy in our bodies has a big impact on us. When we've learned not to 'trust' our bodies, by learning that natural feelings are shameful and should be avoided, we create a body-mind split in ourselves. We learn to distrust our natural impulses and to disconnect from our body, instinct and intuition. When we disconnect from our bodies, from our inner aliveness and our instinctual inner guide, we're left with mental constructs. These are the models of behaviour – that is, good behaviour – that we've learned from our environment.

When it comes to sexuality, this is particularly significant because sexuality is so closely connected to felt sensations in our bodies. When we're left with the images of the mind to understand and express our sexuality, we're torn between society's conflicting messages of sexual suppression and the perpetual sexual readiness from advertisements and porn that we described in the 'Introduction'.

We get a mental image of how our sexuality should express itself rather than an integrated, embodied, felt sense.

Rather than expressing our true selves, we end up having sex limited by the mini-characters we've created in response to society's norms and by what we think is expected of us. Our sexuality becomes an outward thing that is defined by another person or by society's judgments rather than an internal, felt sense finding its natural expression.

When our sexuality is defined and driven
by mental images, we lose connection both
with ourselves and with our partners.

The reason this chapter is called 'Reclaim Your Body' is to make the point that we've somehow lost possession of our body in our culture. For example, think about the way we talk about our relationship with our body as our 'body image'. It's not called our 'body sense' or our 'body experience'. This etymology shows how deeply rooted the split between body and mind is in our culture. We define our relationship with our body using a mental image that describes what we think about it when we compare it with others and how we see our body from the outside – not how we feel it or perceive it as a felt sense.

When body and mind are split in this way,
our bodies become objectified.

This objectification of our bodies isn't something imposed on us by a narcissistic partner who uses our body for their own pleasure. We do it to ourselves. We start judging our own bodies from the perspective of what we could call a 'critical other' – an imagined 'someone else', who is judgemental about our body.

We judge and relate to our body as if it
were an object that was there to enhance our
attractiveness in the eyes of others.

There are other examples: when we get ill, our body is betraying us and we want 'it' to be fixed; when we define our sexuality and our ability (and internal permission) to express ourselves sexually, we judge our body to be either a good or a bad part of us, depending on how we think the other will perceive it; and, most importantly, the mental image that we use as the role model for our judgment is created by what we see – by the media, by advertisements and by porn.

However, the bodies that we see in the media are optimized, perfected and idealized. They are representing images of the body-beautiful that are distorted versions of the masculine and the feminine. What's more, the body images represented in the media, and distilled in porn, display the exact features we've learned to suppress: aggression and sexuality. That's why these images have such a strong pull on us: they're showing us what we're taught to disown internally.

The idealized man is represented as potent, perpetually erect, strong, muscular, ready for aggression (remember – society told us to suppress our anger, even if we still fear 'the dangerous other'). The idealized woman is represented as young and slim (in control, weak, she is not allowed to have a big, powerful body, nor the maturity and wisdom of age and childbirth), and she is highly sexualized with artificially enhanced breasts and swollen lips that make her look as though she has just performed oral sex.

This imagery presents us with stereotypes that have very disempowering and objectifying internal messages. The strong man is controlling the sexuality of the weaker woman while he, in turn, is controlled by his ability to 'perform' – to live up to her sexualized behaviour. This is the downside of porn and of the body images created by media culture.

On the other hand, it's important that we don't fall for the temptation to make porn 'wrong'. Porn is an important outlet for everything we're suppressing in our disowned power, potency and sexuality. Creating a taboo from these perceived shadows is another reason it's highly desirable. In porn we can see the parts of ourselves we're not allowed to feel and express.

When discussing the pros and cons of porn, it's important that we're able to hold both of the following perspectives:

Porn not only represents distorted gender stereotypes and body images, but it also shows us what we're taught to disown in ourselves.

In that sense, porn highlights what is collectively suppressed. We are told by cultural and societal values to suppress and disown aggression and sexuality as felt senses, but that they are permitted within a body image. The smart thing is that in the form of an image, each is perfectly under control. This is the body-mind split in action and the Eros energy tamed.

No wonder we're struggling with our body image in contrast to how we actually feel. No wonder our body image often leaves us disempowered, dried out and impotent when it comes to how we feel in our bodies, how we actually experience ourselves.

The question, therefore, is how can we stop disowning our bodies into an image and disowning our Eros energy as a felt experience? How can we reclaim our bodies? The answer, we would suggest, is beautiful in its simplicity: by feeling – by letting go of our mental images and developing a relationship with our bodies, based on a felt sense. As Fritz Perls, the founder of Gestalt therapy famously said, 'Lose your mind and come to your senses.' Another way of expressing this might be: 'Lose your mind and come into a felt experience of the natural flow of your Eros energy.'

In doing so, we might need to get through a layer of culturally imposed standards of perfection that are keeping our sexuality in control. We might need to let go of our mental images and stop projecting perfection onto our bodies – the voices in our head telling us we're not attractive or perfect enough to be sexual or sexually fulfilled. If we get beyond this we might find a way to experience our bodies as a felt sense that will greatly empower us and empower our freedom of sexual expression.

Exercise: Your Body as Image *(40 minutes)*

This exercise is designed for you to become aware of what you are projecting onto your body image and how that impacts you; a first step in helping you come into a felt relationship with your body.

1. You'll need to make sure you have some private, undisturbed time and that you have your notebook and pencil to hand.

2. Sit in a comfortable position, gently close your eyes and relax into your body. Turn your awareness to your breathing and just notice how it feels to breathe into the body. Take your time.

3. Now turn your awareness to your so-called 'body image' – the relationship you have with your body. What are the thoughts and judgments that usually go through your head when you see your body in a mirror or when you compare yourself to others? Notice both the negative and the positive thoughts.

4. Tune in to something you appreciate about your body, no matter how big or small a body part. Take some time to really appreciate it and feel grateful for it. Imagine you are breathing into that part of your body, and notice how you can generate sensations of pleasure just by turning positive awareness into this place.

5. As you hold on to that in your awareness, tune in to an area of your body that you feel less positive about. What are the challenging areas of your body? Are these perceived imperfections linked to the media stereotypes we described above? Why is it difficult for you to have this specific body feature? What meaning do you give it?

6. Notice how, by giving your perceived imperfection a meaning, you are now judging yourself from the viewpoint of a perceived 'other'. Who is this other? Is it anyone you know – a parent, a peer group, a past or even present lover? Or is it just a fuzzy feeling of 'being outside'?

7. Notice the judgmental words of this other as they criticize you, and how that makes you feel about yourself.

8. Now turn your awareness back into the part of your body you're uncomfortable with. Imagine you are breathing into it and really feel it as you are receiving the critical messages. What do you notice? Does this body part feel like a part of you or does it feel like something 'outside' your body? Are you creating a split between 'you' and your perceived imperfection?

9. Now ask this body part: if it could speak, what would it say? What is its pain, what is its deepest longing? (You might want to remind yourself about the wants, needs and core qualities we discussed in the chapter 'Understand Your Desire', see page 49.)

10. If the needs of this body part were met, how would you feel about yourself? As you imagine this, breathe into this body part and feel how the sensations might change as you direct self-love to this part of your body, integrating it with yourself.

11. When you are ready, gently open your eyes and make notes about what you discovered. In particular, are you objectifying your body and giving away the power of self-love and self-appreciation to a 'critical other'?

The first step to coming into a felt, living and breathing relationship with our body is to realize how much our body image is a mental image created by the 'critical other' – this imagined 'someone else' who is critical about our body. It is gender stereotypes imposed on us by surroundings that we've internalized as critical voices. When these are activated, we disconnect from the aspects of our bodies that we don't like. We avoid seeing and feeling them, we avoid expressing ourselves in a way that would expose our perceived imperfection. This disconnect means that we limit the flow of Eros energy in our bodies and our natural freedom of expression.

This greatly impacts our relationship with our sexuality. Disconnected from the felt sense of our bodies, we look around for role models to teach us what to feel and how to behave, which we find in advertisements, media and porn. Our sexuality becomes an act we play, with the other as the main character, and we end up disempowered by our own mental images. We wait for the other to define our sexuality.

So let's put this straight, as one of the main points of this book:

> *Your sexuality is not defined by your body image. It's the other way round: your body image comes from the relationship you have with your sexuality.*

This means that when we allow ourselves to connect with, and really feel, the erotic energy in our body in its own right, no matter if we have a partner or not, we experience our body in a different way.

> *Allowing the Eros energy to flow in our body will eventually change the way we experience ourselves.*

It connects us with the parts of our bodies that we split off because we're uncomfortable with the way they look. Felt as an internal experience where the 'critical other' is deactivated, we start to embody our bodies.

Many clients we meet in our practice have very critical body images. For them this means that until they've 'sorted that' (lost weight, gained weight, built up muscle mass, removed scars or had plastic surgery), no one will be attracted to them so they can't embrace their sexuality. If we remember the 'critical other' that is speaking in our mind when we judge our body, it becomes very obvious that if we allow our body image to determine if we can be sexual or not, we're giving away all power.

We're waiting for permission from the 'critical other' for us to embrace our sexuality. Again, we're disconnecting from the felt experience of Eros energy. This is a disempowering situation that, sadly, many people experience.

Ironically, this situation will also create the mental images that we have in our minds. When we disconnect from our bodies and don't feel sexually alive, others will pick up on this and won't be attracted to us. Our critical body image and sexual disconnect will become a self-fulfilling prophecy. It doesn't make any difference if we have an active sexual expression, either through regular self-pleasuring or by having sex with a partner or spouse. If we feel shame about self-pleasuring or watching porn, or are trying to hide our bodies during sex, we're denying and suppressing our sexual expression. Eros energy is not owned in our bodies; we feel shame about our sexual self, which means others will sense this and find us less attractive.

It's not about how our bodies look, but how we are with our bodies.

If there's no Eros energy allowed, we'll feel unattractive to ourselves and consequently to others. If we allow Eros energy to be flowing freely, others will feel our aliveness and will want to connect with it. In other words, in order for us to reclaim our bodies, we need to be turned on by ourselves.

We need to let Eros energy flow freely in our bodies.

However, being turned on by ourselves does not mean aiming for a body image that satisfies the 'critical other' so that, when comparing ourselves to media-induced gender stereotypes, we find ourselves 'attractive enough' to feel sexual.

It's completely the opposite. Being turned on by ourselves means connecting with our innate sexual energy.

Our innate sexual energy is an energy that no one can give to us and no one can take away. It is ours.

Being turned on by ourselves means getting to know the pleasures and subtle sensations of our own bodies. This doesn't include the use of porn or other external stimulants. It's not about what you think you're supposed to feel – the expectations that you put on yourself – but the concrete, actual experience.

THE ANATOMY OF PLEASURE – EROGENOUS ZONES

As we described in the chapter 'Understand Your Desire' (see page 49), most people believe that sex means an activity between two (or more) people, that it includes the genitals and that penetration in some form is mostly involved. As we explained, sex is an energy that moves between sensual and sexual expression, and has a 'you know it when you feel it' quality to its variety of expression.

In the last chapter's exercise, 'Self-Pleasuring in a New Way' (see page 98), we showed you how sexual energy and pleasure can be felt in the whole body, not only in the genitals. Adding to that, you've probably heard that the body consists of what we call primary and secondary erogenous zones. An erogenous zone is a part of the body that has many nerve endings that stimulate our sexual response – the flow of our Eros energy.

The primary erogenous zones are the lips, tongue, nipples and areas of the genitals: for men these are the foreskin, glans and corona of the penis, the prostate and the anus; for women these are the clitoris, vulva and anus. Stimulation of the primary erogenous zones will connect to an explicitly sexual energy.

The secondary erogenous zones are connected to a more sensual response. These include many more areas of the body, such as the face, neck, hair, ears, inside of the elbows, navel area, outer labia, other areas of the penis not defined above, inner thighs and so on. Even though these areas most immediately connect to a sensual response, their stimulation can also create a sexual reaction.

Sexual pleasure, then, comes from the entire body, not just the genitals. When we let go of the idea that sexual pleasure equals genital stimulation, we can start reconnecting with our entire body as an entire erogenous zone. This is a real game-changer.

> *If we perceive sex as being about genital stimulation,*
> *we tend to pursue only the increasing intensity*
> *of the sexual energy, while sensual energy only*
> *counts as the foreplay for the 'real thing'.*

This means we become goal-oriented and focused on reaching an orgasm, and probably often perform for ourselves or our partner, that is we become more concerned about how we appear than how we feel.

> *This pursuit of intensity means we tend to lose the capacity*
> *to feel the subtle energies and sensations in our body.*

Not only is the moment lost towards an end goal, but an internal dialogue of *will I/they orgasm or not?* will very probably activate a critical voice in our mind, which makes the body less likely to experience orgasm.

By feeling the innate sexual response, rather than thinking it, by slowing down and including the subtle sensations from our secondary erogenous zones, our whole bodies become alive. This inevitably changes our relationship with our body image. Remember, our relationship with our sexuality defines our body image – not the other way around.

We start liking ourselves when we have a positive, embodied, felt experience with ourselves. When we're ashamed of – and therefore disconnected from – our bodies, we don't give attention or awareness to the subtle sensations of pleasure we're able to experience from the secondary erogenous zones. The trick here is to turn the wheel and do it anyway: touch yourself, get to know yourself, discover what's good from a felt perspective, enjoy your whole body's capacity for pleasure, and from this get into a living, breathing, felt and pleasure-based relationship with your body. Time to play!

Exercise: Love Your Body *(45 minutes)*

This exercise is a variation of the self-pleasure exercise in the previous chapter, but this time our focus will be on having a felt experience of your body from the place of loving, present touch. When you start generating that energy in yourself instead of waiting for someone to give it to you, your relationship with your body image will change.

For this exercise you'll need a blindfold or a soft scarf to be able to cover your eyes. You should also read through the whole exercise now, as you will be blindfolded further on.

I. Make sure that you have some undisturbed time on your own. Prepare the room for a love encounter – as a sensual, welcoming environment. Light some candles, scented perhaps, and make sure the room is warm and cosy. We don't suggest playing music during this exercise as you should stay focused on yourself.

2. Still fully clothed, sit down on a bed or mattress, and gently blindfold yourself. Take a few moments to breathe gently into your body and feel yourself.

3. Now gently place both hands on your heart, and breathe into your heart for a few moments. Feel how your heart responds when you make contact with it. Imagine that you're making an invisible connection between your heart and your hands, like threads of energy running from your heart and into your hands. Notice how your hands become alive, filled with sensation, just because you turn your loving awareness to them.

4. Now, very, very slowly start moving your fingers. Let your fingertips feel each other. Let your hands feel each other. Feel the vast richness

of sensation in your hands as they explore each other as if for the first time.

5. Let your hands slowly explore your body, as you're still fully clothed. Move your hands as slowly as you can, feeling the richness of the different sensations as you touch different body parts, different volumes and different surfaces.

6. Now imagine you're your own first lover, so start very slowly undressing yourself with the loving, compassionate excitement of each new sensation as you go. Feel the pleasure under your fingertips as your hands make their way to your skin.

7. As you gradually undress, feel how every part of your body responds to your loving touch. Breathe into the sensation, and use the breath to make contact with the body part that you are touching. Notice how the sensation increases.

8. Let your hands find their way, and stay with the sensations of each touch, as if you were touching yourself for the first time. Avoid going into a self-pleasuring routine, but stay with the gentle, conscious, loving touch.

9. Breathe fully into your body and feel how that increases the sensation: the more you become fully present with the touch, the more self-love you are able to experience.

10. When you've woken up the whole of your body, gently place one hand on your heart and one on your genitals. Feel the connection between them. Take your time.

11. Speak out loud the following affirmation with a deep voice, fully felt in your body: 'I love my sexual body.' Repeat until you really feel it.

12. When you feel ready, gently remove the blindfold and take your time to come back to the room. Make some notes in your sketchbook about the experience.

OWNERSHIP OF YOUR BODY

In this exercise we deactivated the 'critical other' so we could come into a felt, heart-based relationship with our body. When the 'critical other' is activated we go into our mind and judge our body from a mental image of our body, which very rarely lives up to idealized cultural stereotypes. Often we end up feeling shame or self-criticism, which makes us disconnect from our body, unable to feel the subtle sensation of Eros energy already present.

When we use our whole body as a playground
for pleasure and sensation, not having to
perform for anyone or for an orgasm but
just feeling the natural flow of Eros energy,
we become alive within ourselves.

We don't have to look towards the 'critical other' to have a relationship with our body. In a felt experience we'll be less dependent on the body image and be more grounded.

As sex therapists, we are advocating a whole new way of engaging with your body, to take back from the 'critical other' the right to opine about your body, the right to a felt experience and to real ownership of your body – because you are in it and you know how good that feels.

To take ownership of your body means first
acknowledging not only that you have a
body, but also that you are a body.

This is a radically different approach from what we're used to in the way we manage our bodies – how we look after our failing bodies when we get ill, or mostly feeling, as one client described herself, like 'a brain in a jar'. In this more empowered approach, we're inviting you to embody yourself and take full responsibility, in a deep sense.

Your body is not an external part that belongs to you. What if, instead, it's the other way around – you belong to your body? There aren't two parts, there is one.

We are advocating the experience of yourself and the world *through* your body. To know that body and mind are one, and that one of these parts is just another aspect of the other. This is taking full responsibility for being one with your body. And equally, if some part of the body is hurting or ill, it's not your body that needs healing: it's you.

YOUR BODY CARRIES YOUR STORY

Another way to experience the world through your body, and to fully own it, is to know that your body carries your history. Every experience that we've had, and every emotion that we've felt, is stored in the body. Somatic therapies and bodywork traditions such as our own therapeutic modality Psychosexual Somatics®, bioenergetics, Rolfing®, Rosen Method, craniosacral therapy and even conventional massage are all based on the same knowledge about emotional and energetic blocks that have turned into patterns of tension in the body. Our facial expressions, our wrinkles, our body posture, the composition and structure of our limbs and body parts, where we hold tension and where we're deflated, where we put on body fat or muscles, and even how sexual energy runs in our body – these all come down to how emotions are stored in our body.

Physical similarities with our parents will most likely include a reflection of thought patterns and beliefs that we've unconsciously inherited. We're not just susceptible to a random, genetic blueprint: there's the blueprint that forms the potential, and there are our beliefs that form the physical actualization.

This means that the way our bodies look is a product of beliefs and experiences that we've had.

When we're projecting a negative body image onto our body, there's something about ourselves that we disown. We blame our body because it's too difficult for us to take ownership of the emotion. If there's a part or the whole of our body that we dislike, we need to ask, *What is it in myself that I am blaming on my body? What is my body telling me about my internal belief about myself?*

Chances are we'll find that most of our negative stories about ourselves originate in our childhood:

Namely, we weren't seen, loved or accepted enough, or in the way we needed it, and developed a negative self-image that might have kept affirming itself through our adult life. We came to believe that, deep down, we weren't adequately worthy, important, attractive, intelligent, interesting or capable and so on. While most of us have found ways to cover up our insecurities by being successful in other areas, the relationship we have with our body still holds the belief and the memory. In that sense, when we say that our body carries our story, we mean that our body carries the stories and messages we're telling ourselves – our history as the internal belief that has become our story. Our body is therefore a perfect reflection of who we think we are. To own our body also means to own our history.

Of course, our body also carries our physical history. Fitness, diet, childbirth, ageing, scars, illnesses, stress, sleeplessness, sunbathing, tobacco, alcohol and so on are all factors well known to impact how our body looks.

Some of it is caused by choices we've made, and some of it has happened to us, but it's all a part of the truth about who we are.

Let's recall Keats' famous words:

Beauty is truth, truth beauty. That is all
Ye know on earth, and all ye need to know.
FROM *ODE ON A GRECIAN URN* BY JOHN KEATS, 1819

Beauty, in this sense, is authenticity: being who we are, in the fullness of our humanness, with our wrinkles, scars, rolls and flaws, because that is what makes us who we are and what gives us depth. In this sense, Barbie-doll type perfection is not beautiful, but a woman expressing her authentic self is. Such a woman is owning the history of her life and her body without shame. She is letting the authentic beauty of her being shine through.

Diana's Story

Diana is a 32-year-old woman who came to see us because she was experiencing difficulties in sex and relationships. She appeared attractive, with rounded curves, but described herself as 'fat with big legs'. She grew up in an open-minded community where nakedness was quite common. She described her mother as disempowered in her feminine, and her father as a dominating male energy: he would call Diana 'lazy' and would often say that she had a 'fat bottom'. Despite her lovely appearance and a graceful, confident energy around her, she had never been in a relationship, and had experienced only unsatisfactory or even decidedly bad sexual encounters.

It was clear that her body image was very negative, and that she had internalized her father's judgments as the 'critical other'. Furthermore, the environment in which she grew up, which she had experienced as being without any boundaries and slightly sexualized, had fostered her own counter-response: she would feel hugely intimidated by nakedness, especially in men. She had very efficiently learned to suppress her own Eros energy because of shame about her body, and because Eros energy also had associations with unbounded behaviour.

Deprived of her own Eros energy, she couldn't feel herself in a positive way and had lost connection with her body, which had become an enemy. She wasn't anchored in a positive sense of self through a felt experience but was reliant on comparing herself to others and to the idealized body image produced by mass media. This negative view, of criticized body image and suppressed Eros energy, made it hard for her to be intimate with other people. She had learned to suppress her negative emotions by coming across as strong-willed and confident, but just behind that surface was a deep resentment towards herself that didn't allow anyone to come near her.

During the course of our work she began to understand her anger and her feeling of being unsafe around men that originated in her childhood experiences. She understood that intimate situations triggered old patterns of defence against past abusive experiences. This was hugely liberating, because it enabled her to stay with the 'here and now', the reality of her current experience. She learned to connect to her body and to feel the sensations of each touch, each moment, and in this way she could decide whether she was safe or not, if she wanted to allow intimacy or if she needed to put up a healthy boundary. As we found ways for her to express the negative emotions she had built up since childhood, she was less often triggered to keep people at a distance. Gradually she was able to allow herself intimacy and positive sexual experiences. Most importantly in this context, though, the more she got in touch with her Eros energy, the more her relationship with her body image changed. In her owns words:

'Due to our work, I have discovered that I am actually not as bad as I thought, and I have understood where all these negative patterns come from. And now I don't need them any more. I don't have to bother about others' critical voices (especially my parents') any more. Yes, I still don't have the kind of figure I want to have, but the rest of me is very, very okay. It is not about me controlling myself and having to be perfect so that I am good enough to connect with people and be loved, but about me daring to be who I am, and that has nothing to do with others.'

When rooted in oneself as a felt, embodied experience connected to our Eros energy and not depending on others to 'give it to us' either by permission or acknowledgement, engrained negative stories fall apart and we're able to be present, loving and accepting of ourselves.

• •

ON NUDITY

Sadly, in our society we have a slightly distorted relationship with nudity.

Our discomfort with nudity arises
partly from our body shame, partly
from our disowned sexuality.

Both can be crippling for our sense of self. As we saw from Diana's case (above), shame about her own body had been passed on to her, and she had also experienced nakedness as intimidating and sexualized.

Idealized body images are promoted by mass media and create an internal judgment, but we have nowhere to turn to for a natural relationship with our body. It's as if nudity means sex; if we're naked we're looking for sex. There is a great loss in this.

When we disown our nakedness, we disown our body. We're sending a clear message to our body that 'You're not allowed to be here' – that the naked body is shameful and should remain hidden. The result is that we deprive ourselves of the feeling of embodiment that allows our Eros energy to flow freely.

It's only when we're comfortable with our nakedness
that we're fully able to feel our own bodies.

Let's make a very important distinction here. To be in touch with our Eros energy doesn't mean we need to express ourselves sexually; no more than nudity indicates that we want to have sex. Our Eros energy is our life-force energy. It informs everything that we are and do, no matter what activity we're engaged in. Eros energy is the aliveness of our bodies. It's very important for us to fully own the fact that as human beings we are sexual beings – because we are, no matter how efficiently we try to split off our sexuality.

However, being a sexual being does not mean that we want to express ourselves sexually at any given moment.

It's simply a fact of owning our human nature. This is hugely important because by owning our sexual nature we also know when nakedness or sexual behaviour is consensual and appropriate and when it's not. In Scandinavia, for example, naked winter bathing is a popular activity, and people of all genders and all ages enjoy the sauna and swimming in a relaxed and nonsexual environment. Nakedness does not mean sex, and sexual energy can be contained in a natural and respectful way because it's not suppressed in the environment and because the boundaries are clear.

At the same time, in many other parts of the world this kind of public nakedness would be unthinkable. For many people, sleeping in full pyjamas is normal, which creates the alienation of the body.

Not even in our private sleep are we allowed to have a relationship with our body.

This is hugely disempowering. We've internalized the societal control over our bodies, allowing it to penetrate deep into our intimate being. We feel shame and awkwardness when we don't have an idealized image to hide behind, and cover up the 'inappropriateness' of our natural bodies because we cannot make a distinction between nakedness and sex.

This is a vicious circle: the fewer natural, naked bodies we see, the more we rely on media stereotypes for comparison, which will make us reject our own body.

And the more we reject our body, the more we reject our sexual energy. Disowning our own sexual energy is what makes us vulnerable to overstepping either other people's boundaries or our own because we don't feel, we don't know who we are, and therefore rely on mental images and beliefs passed on to us by parents, religion and society.

The way back to an empowered relationship with our sexuality, and to loving our bodies as a felt sense emanating from inside and out, is to get to know how our body feels and to listen to its stories; to own our bodies' natural sexual energy, to enjoy it, but to be conscious about where and how we express that.

A wonderful place to start is the most simple: sleep naked. Get to know how you feel. Honour the histories that your body is carrying and the energy that is flowing through it in each and every moment. And enjoy it.

KEY 4:
BE PRESENT

The essence of 'real sex' is embodiment. A lot of sex happens in the body and if you're mainly in your mind, chances are you're not having great sex.

Unfortunately, as we've seen in the chapter 'The Pros and Cons of Pornography' (see page 23), if you actively watch porn, its powerful images operate as a great distraction from being 'present'.

Perhaps the lure of these images is so potent because they represent our idealized fantasies; perhaps because they are associated with the intense biochemical releases that happen during orgasm. For so many people, pornographic images are deeply imprinted within their brains and are activated once more during sex. This means that during sex with a real person there can be a tendency to revert to those images rather than be present with the person you're actually with.

Even if you're not actively using porn yourself, it is virtually impossible not to be aware of it. Whether we watch porn or not, it exerts its influence over our cultural norms and the imagery that our culture uses for sexuality.

When this happens, we're not having sex or making love to the person we're in bed with, but with a mental movie we're playing in our head. That movie might give us specific imagery – body shape, fantasy scenario, the person we want to be having sex with in that fantasy and so on. Or the movie may be a blurred version of what we feel are the expectations from sex. These could be expectations that we place upon ourselves or that we want others to live up to. These expectations from pornography could include having a strong erection, trying specific sexual positions (even if you're not enjoying them), making a lot of sexual sounds, orgasming (perhaps simultaneously with your partner) or having an insatiable desire and willing readiness for sex at all times.

> *While it's not wrong to have fantasies during sex or to revert to mental imagery, it's important to recognize that the moment we do so we lose contact with the person we're having sex with.*

Equally importantly, we lose contact with our own bodily sensations, which are an essential part of a positive sexual experience.

BEING IN THE BODY

In order to have great, 'real sex', it's important to be present with your partner in an embodied way, still remaining in the experience of your body and not getting lost in your mind. However, most people tend to come out of their body during sex, with a strong tendency to be in their heads.

> *What goes on inside the person's head during sex varies, of course, but this essential disconnection from the body is one of the key factors that create problems in sexual intimacy.*

Some people are caught up in fantasies of what they wish their sexual experience to look like; some are lost to pressure they put on themselves to perform or to look a certain way that they believe is 'sexy'. A lot of this mental imagery arises from pornography. Some people have a self-critical voice telling them they won't look good if they lose too much control during sex or make too much sound. Some even think about completely unrelated things, such as what they will have for supper tomorrow.

There's also another group of people, who come out of their bodies completely during sex because they don't feel their body is a safe place to inhabit during sex. The most obvious reason for this is that the person has suffered some kind of sexual abuse or trauma in their history. If that's you, it's important to know that fears you hold about sex can be resolved. The anxiety that you may have about being in your body during sex can be transformed quite easily with somatic (body-based) psychotherapy.

Resolving sexual trauma is beyond the scope of this book, but it's something we deal with in our psychotherapeutic practice on an almost daily basis. A person can usually quickly transform their experience of sex and begin to enjoy it by using a combination of mental awareness, mindfulness and body-based practices such as our own approach, Psychosexual Somatics®.

Meanwhile, many people come out of their bodies because the body is the storehouse of our emotions.

Emotions are called feelings because we 'feel' them in the body.

When a client sits in our therapy rooms and tells us they feel sad or angry, we often ask them how they know that they feel those things in that moment. The answer almost always refers to physical sensation. If someone is sad they may feel tightness in their chest or a lump in their throat. If they are angry they may report a rush of energy up the front of their body or tension in their arms or jaw. A knot in their stomach may mean fear or anxiety.

If we learn, usually in childhood, that feelings are not allowed – if we're told to 'grow up' when we express our vulnerability or that 'big boys don't cry' and so on – then there may be a tendency to avoid feeling our emotions. We might even have received that message in subtler ways, simply by witnessing that our parents didn't express emotions, or that our emotions weren't listened to, considered or cared about. This would hold true for both so-called positive and negative emotions. Many people learn that spontaneous outbursts of positive emotions aren't allowed; that it's shameful, self-indulgent, selfish or just unimportant. This will definitely impact our capacity to allow feelings of deep pleasure and orgasmic bliss.

> *If we've learned not to feel, we'll most likely*
> *tend to stay out of our body in sex.*

Our body will be holding emotions we don't want to surface and we'll therefore maintain the disconnection.

Additionally, most of us experience feelings of inadequacy at some point when it comes to sex itself. Whether it's about how we look or our technique, not feeling good enough about sex is something that plagues most people at some time in their sexual lives. Good looks are no bar to these feelings, either. It can be easy to think that if someone is physically attractive they must be sexually confident. In reality, the many extremely beautiful people we've met in our clinic have included some of the least sexually secure.

SHAME-BUSTING

We may experience other uncomfortable emotions during sex. The most prevalent of these is shame. Sadly, despite the ubiquitous nature of sexual imagery in our culture, sex and shame still go hand in hand for many people.

> *Shame is the most powerful inhibitor to 'real sex'.*

We may have learned early on that 'good girls don't' or that 'sex is dirty'. Perhaps we naturally and curiously explored our bodies as children and were told off for touching ourselves. Maybe our innocent games of doctors and nurses during childhood were greeted with derision or made 'wrong' in some way. For some it can be as simple as a little girl taking off her top on a hot day because the boys around her did the same and being told that she is a naughty girl for uncovering herself. For others, sexual suppression and the strongest messages we received about sex are from our adolescence, where we might have experienced control or shaming about our natural curiosity to express our beauty or our innocent, emerging sexuality. If we had same-sex desires, the shame and suppression might have been even stronger.

Whatever the reason, every one of us has probably experienced feelings of shame around our sexual self-expression at some point in our lives.

Shame is a crippling emotion. It can make us want to curl up and hide or become frozen in panic. We might wish that the earth would swallow us up and that we're not seen. Shame runs a story – another mental movie – which tells us 'I'm not okay.' It's the feeling that arises when we believe we've done something 'wrong' or when we want to do something that we judge as 'wrong'. Shame is the death knell of great sex.

As we discussed in the chapter 'Know Your Sexual Self' (see page 75), every fantasy – even the ones you feel most shameful about – has at its core a deeper gift, a beautiful quality that can be experienced through the gateway of your fantasy. However, feelings of shame can persist and are among the main blocks to letting us be in the body during sex.

But by remaining in your body during sex and recognizing that you are safe to do so, you'll be able to enjoy more physical pleasure and connect more deeply with your partner.

Remember, your partner isn't inside your head, so if that's where you are during sex, you're on your own.

You can't connect with your partner from your mind. Your mind is a useful tool for reflecting on the past, planning for the future and for working things out using logic – but what your mind can't do is to feel. It can't experience sensations or emotions and it can't connect with others – each of these things is felt through our senses, not worked out with the mind. To experience them you need to be in your body.

Let's help you to become more aware of what's actually going on in your body.

Exercise: Body Scanning *(20 minutes)*

This exercise is designed to help you to become aware of the sensory experience of the body in a neutral state – when you are resting and feeling calm. We'll be focusing on helping you to bring your awareness into your body and simply to feel what is going on in there.

1. Find a time when you won't be interrupted and make sure you are sitting or lying comfortably, with your notebook and pen within reach. Take some nice slow, deep breaths down into your abdomen and let your exhalation be slow and easy. Don't force the breath, just allow it to deepen as you breathe more fully into your body.

2. Once you begin to feel your breath and start to relax, you can start scanning your body for sensations. Begin at the soles of your feet – bring your awareness to them and notice how they feel. Are you aware of the fabric clothing them, and maybe a tingling sensation as you're feeling this part of your body? Can you tell if they're relaxed or if some muscles are tense in them? Do they feel hot or cool?

3. Now move your awareness to the feet themselves. Notice if your toes are curled up or relaxed. Again, become aware of temperature and sensations on the skin and so on.

4. Move your awareness slowly up your body to your ankles, then to your calves and shins. Let your attention rest with each new area for a few moments as you observe the physical sensations in your body.

5. Gradually move your awareness up your legs and into your pelvis. Notice how you feel as you bring your awareness into this part of yourself. Does it feel exciting or uncomfortable to consciously focus on your sex centre, in and around your genitals?

6. As you bring your awareness into your torso, you may begin to notice emotional feelings as well as physical sensations. There's no need to try to change these emotions or make them go away. Just be aware of them and notice if any particular emotion comes up when you bring your awareness to any particular body part.

7. Continue scanning upwards and include your diaphragm, then your chest and heart area, in your awareness. Focus your attention on your spine as well, and notice any areas there where you holding tightness.

8. Bring your focus up to your shoulders. Are you trying to control things by keeping them tight or are they relaxed and soft?

9. Continue moving your awareness higher up your body, into your neck and throat. Does your throat feel free and open or is it holding on tightly, feeling a bit closed and tense?

10. Include the muscles in your face and in your mouth. Be aware of your tongue and the root of your tongue. See if bringing awareness to it helps them to soften.

11. Finally, notice the muscles of your scalp and around the top of your head.

12. Once you've completed the body scan, you can bring your attention back to your breath and just let its natural rhythm soothe you.

13. When you are fully back in the room, make a few notes on what you noticed during this exercise. Did you discover parts of your body that were tense, which you hadn't realized beforehand? Did you find that emotions came up for you when you concentrated on certain parts of your body?

14. Acknowledge whether you kept coming into your head and thinking about unrelated things. Maybe you heard a voice in your head telling you that this is stupid or that you are not doing it right.

Each of the thoughts or judgments you noticed in the exercise are distractions to being present. Every time you came back into your head with a thought about something other than what was happening in your body in that moment, you lost connection with what was actually happening and you stopped being present.

It is a challenging exercise for many of us. Most of us have learned that our mind is good but the body is an uncomfortable and perhaps scary place to be, so we've conditioned ourselves to revert back to our heads whenever we can.

Staying with what's actually happening in your body, without coming back to thoughts in your head, takes practice – but the payoff is the ability to have really amazing 'real sex'.

USING MINDFULNESS

Mindfulness has become a buzzword in the psychotherapy and personal development fields in recent years. It's simply the practice of observing what is happening in the moment, helping us to become be more aware of our thoughts, feelings and sensations. Since mindfulness is way to focus us on being present with the 'now', it's one of the most powerful tools we have for developing our ability to have 'real sex'.

Leading neuroscientist Daniel Siegel states that the regular practice of mindfulness helps in 'regulating our bodies, attuning to others, having emotional balance, calming fear, pausing before acting, having insight and empathy, being moral in our thinking and our actions, and having more access to intuition'[11] – all skills that we need to develop in order to allow more intimacy into our lives. These are the powerful effects that can be gained from simply bringing your awareness to something and observing it without judgment.

> *Mindfulness is effectively a form of meditation but without the spiritual trappings that put many people off.*

Spiritual traditions have understood mindfulness for millennia, especially in the East, where meditation has been practised most widely until recent times. Now the age-old wisdom of philosophies such as Buddhism and Hinduism are gaining ground in the West, not only as spiritual practices but as tools for psychological growth and personal self-development.

There are many studies that demonstrate that both meditation and mindfulness, when practised regularly, not only increase our sense of wellbeing and help us to feel calmer and more peaceful; they also physically change the neural pathways in our brain, increasing the number of nerve cells (neurons) in the vagus nerve, the primary nerve responsible for our ability to rest and relax.

One form of mindfulness is to focus on your thoughts and simply observe them as you sit or lie quietly. This can be helpful in raising awareness of your thought processes and mental beliefs. This is all part of increasing awareness, which, as we noted at the start of the book, is one of our golden rules for self-development work.

You tried a variation on mindfulness in the previous exercise where we invited you to focus on your bodily sensations and on any emotional feelings you noticed as you did so. Since this practice is about what you felt in your body, we call it somatic mindfulness. 'Somatic' simply means 'relating to the body', and because the body is so integral to sex it's essential that we learn to focus our attention on the body and notice, without judgment, what arises for us during the process.

FAST-FORWARDING

One of the strategies that most of us have for avoiding staying present is 'fast-forwarding'. Anyone who has watched pornography has probably fast-forwarded to the interesting bits, whatever that means for him or her. If you do this you will miss the build up to whatever climactic scene you are aiming for. Sadly, people not only do this while watching pornography but also during sex with others.

Instead of staying with what is actually happening in the moment, our minds start to race forward and our mental movie gets ahead of what is really going on – it starts to predict or plan for what it thinks should come next. Perhaps you noticed this in the exercise you just did. When you scanned up your body, did you find parts where you didn't want to spend time? Or perhaps your mind told you, *This is boring. I know what's coming next. Let's move on.*

> **Fast-forwarding is one of the most commonly used avoidance strategies in sex.**

By fast-forwarding, we may avoid many different things. It's very common to use this strategy, unconsciously, to avoid being present with our experience or with our feelings or even with our partners during sex. This is a guaranteed way to ensure unfulfilling sex.

As therapists, we've found that there are a couple of very common types of fast-forwarding; they are broad generalizations but they are generally true. The first is in men (for the most part), where the impulse is usually to rush ahead to what they want to happen next: 'Enough foreplay, let's get to the main event,' is the fast-forwarding story running in many men's (and some women's) minds. It's as though, caught up by the sexual energy impulse that feels the need to 'get somewhere' and is predominately genitally focused, we struggle with staying with what is happening in the moment and we fast-forward our mental movie to 'something more interesting'.

Fast-forwarding brings us into the future before it has happened and therefore stops us being in the present.

As our mind races ahead, it leaves the body standing still and disconnected. It avoids us feeling the erotic tension that builds up during sex and wants to discharge itself.

There are two negative effects from fast-forwarding to what we want to happen next. The first is that we stop being with what is going on, and in doing so we lose connection with our body and its potentially pleasurable sensations. We also lose connection with our partner, since they are not in our mind but either in their body or in their own mental movie. The only chance we have of coming into connection with our partner is to be present, but this can't happen if we switch into our mental movie.

The second type of fast-forwarding is around orgasm. This happens when people focus on orgasm as a goal of sex. It's especially prevalent for women who have difficulties with orgasm. Often the feeling of arousal is there, sensation builds up and they may feel themselves close to where they imagine orgasm is, as though it's hiding just around the next bend. In their enthusiasm to reach that goal (remember, orgasm is not in fact the goal of 'real sex'), they momentarily lose connection with themselves and their bodily sensation, by fast-forwarding. This is usually disastrous for orgasm.

The more we focus on chasing orgasm, the further away it gets, and it will always outrun us if we think like this.

Another version of fast-forwarding around orgasm is for women who have either very little sensation in their vagina and therefore find it difficult to enjoy penetration, or women who just never reach orgasm, either clitoral or vaginal. Sadly, we can report from our client practice that such problems affect a huge number of women. Either they choose to fake orgasm or it has become a silent understanding in the relationship that this won't happen, least not during penetration. In both cases, she just wants to get penetration over and done with as fast as possible, or bring any unsatisfying sex to an end, and is rushing her partner to orgasm. This approach is, of course, deadening for good, connective sex. By contrast, it can also be very tempting to fast-forward to orgasm when in the moment because the feeling of orgasm is so delicious and exciting that part of us wants to rush there as fast as possible.

Whether we're chasing orgasm or have given up on it, instead of rushing towards it we need to stay present with the moment, relax into the sensations that are there and allow the orgasm to find us.

Alison's Story

Alison was a typical example of how negatively fast-forwarding can impact your life. She was in her mid-thirties and she enjoyed sex. She was open-minded, happy to explore different sexual scenarios and even enjoyed playing out sexual fantasies with partners. She had never experienced abuse or sexual trauma. However, she had a problem that plagued her intimate life. She was able quite easily to experience orgasm when alone, through self-pleasuring, but found it impossible to orgasm when with a partner.

Over the years she had found that, since partners experienced her as sexually open, they expected her to be able to orgasm. They often took it as a personal affront that they could not get her to orgasm. It sometimes made her partners feel inadequate and it made Alison feel that there was something sexually wrong with her. Since she enjoyed sex in general, she could not understand what was going wrong. She tried faking orgasm with a few partners, and although they never found out, she didn't feel good about this. It just compounded her feeling that there was something wrong with her.

In therapy, she understood that her resistance to orgasming when with a partner was about a fear of losing control. Orgasm is an act of letting go, a loss of mental and physical control that can feel scary for many people.

Alison realized that although she was very turned on in sex and quickly got aroused, when she came close to orgasming she flipped out of her bodily sensations and into her mental movie of having an orgasm. She fast-forwarded the last stage of the build-up towards orgasm when she was having sex with someone else and in doing so she lost connection with herself – and her orgasm. Her mental imagery was also governed by what she thought men wanted her to look like in sex – drawn largely from pornographic images. As she said, 'I made myself look like the porn star I thought they wanted me to be.'

Having learned from us that she should try to come back to her body during sex and away from her mental imagery, Alison was able to slow down both her mind and body and after a few months she was able to have her first orgasm with a sexual partner. Switching off her fast-forward button during sex required awareness, but once Alison understood what she was doing wrong, she was able to begin changing her behaviour.

. . . .

THE CHALLENGE OF SPONTANEITY

Another effect of fast-forwarding is that it stops us from being spontaneous. Spontaneity is one of the keys to 'real sex' and one that most people find surprisingly tricky.

If we fast-forward, we're making a judgement about what should happen next or what we wish would happen next. By being out of the present moment and creating that sense of expectation, we both apply performance pressure on ourselves and, by trying to predict what will happen, limit what this might be.

Such predictions are, by definition, predefined. By telling ourselves, *This is what should happen next*, we stop anything else being able to occur. Sex is most real and most enjoyable when we allow it to emerge naturally and follow its own ebb and flow. As soon as we start to make a route map of what sex is meant to look like, we limit that flow. Instead, we could imagine sex as a vast oceanic potential: almost anything can happen in it. Different moods or feelings may come and go. Different 'mini-characters' may come to the fore or recede. We might feel that we want to move between sexual and sensual energies or we might want to stay in one more than the other. Part of the pleasure and excitement of sex is not knowing what it will look and feel like, spontaneously allowing whatever energy is there in the moment to flow. If we always knew what would happen next, sex would quickly become boring.

Imagine that you're making love to a long-time sexual partner. Each move is known in advance: the type of sensation you are going to have; the parts of your body that will be explored or ignored; that one touch will lead to another, which will lead to penetration and so on. The quality of energy that you each bring will always be the same. Even though both parties may reach orgasm, in the long run this type of sex usually ends up being unsatisfying for both of you.

If we always make love in the same way, it will lose its appeal and certainly its excitement.

For so many people, this is exactly how sex feels. Spontaneity so often gets lost in long-term relationships. We work out a game plan we think works for both parties and we stick to it, no matter what. 'If it worked once, it'll work again,' we tell ourselves. We become lazy and unimaginative. Ultimately this lack of excitement will lead to a decline in sexual drive. After all, why would you want to keep having sex if it became boring? This is one of the reasons that understanding mini-characters is so important for great 'real sex'. If we can move between different sexual mini-characters, we can enjoy different types of sex, with a different quality of energy, almost every time.

The problem with spontaneity is that it can feel uncomfortable. If we know what's coming next we can plan for it, prepare for it and in doing so have some sense of control over it. Losing control was what scared Alison. If we try something new in sex, we risk rejection or feeling shame. We have a sexual impulse but we block it by not expressing it. This is more of the editing-out that goes on all the time in sex. Understanding that fast-forwarding is one way to avoid the risks in being spontaneous makes a good start to changing that pattern into something that allows more connection and embodiment.

By being present with what we're really feeling in each moment and by noticing the impulses in our body, we can bring the aliveness back to our sexual experiences and to even the most long-standing of relationships. The start of this process is somatic mindfulness, which you experienced in the first exercise in this chapter (see page 126). By practising this exercise several times, you will begin to notice what goes on in your body in neutral situations, such as when you are resting and relaxing. Once you've begun to get the hang of this, you can take things to the next level and start exploring erotic mindfulness.

With erotic mindfulness you can practise
being spontaneous with yourself.

Exercise: Erotic Mindfulness (45 minutes)

In this exercise we invite you to self-pleasure while noticing each moment that you flip into your head and lose connection with your body. Whether you start to fast-forward or move into fantasy, notice voices of judgment or self-criticism, or something else. Be aware of anything that takes you out of being fully present in your body.

I.   Make sure you have some quiet time where you won't be interrupted and that you have your notebook and pen nearby. Prepare yourself for a self-pleasuring session in whichever way feels most sensual and relaxed for you, without using porn or fantasy. Stay present with yourself and your own experience.

2. Start with completing Steps 1–12 of the 'Body Scanning' exercise (see page 126) to come into full connection with your body.

3. Now begin to touch your body in a way that gives you pleasure. To begin with, don't touch your genitals or other obvious erogenous zones, but let your hands stroke your belly, arms, legs, hair and head, for example.

4. Allow your body to move. Staying still stops sexual energy from moving, so give yourself permission to move your spine, legs and pelvis. Notice any internal judgments as you do so.

5. Breathe and make sound. Notice how you feel as you do this. Can you allow yourself to move and make sound or do you tend to freeze, tense your muscles and clamp your jaw shut?

6. Gradually include the areas of your body you find more erogenous, without ignoring the parts you've already given attention to. Do not focus exclusively on the genitals, but allow them to be included in the touch.

7. Notice how you feel as more sexual energy builds. Do you stay focused on your pleasure or do thoughts and judgments pop into your head? Do you get lost in pursuing an orgasm or can you allow your body to find its pleasure in each moment?

8. Once the energy reaches a certain level of pleasure or excitement, do you start to feel uncomfortable? Do you have thoughts about how you might be judged if you were seen having that much sexual energy?

9. Do this exercise for at least 20 minutes, without any goal except noticing how it feels and what stops you from being fully present in your body during the experience. Are you able to stay present or do you get lost in thoughts, in self-criticism or fast-forwarding?

10. As soon as you find yourself losing connection with your body, gently bring your awareness back to the sensations in your body. Remember to be gentle with yourself and lovingly invite your attention back to the physical, felt experience that your body is having.

11. When the exercise feels complete, gently bring yourself back, thank your body for the pleasures it offered you and make some notes about your observations.

Try this exercise daily for a week or more. The more you practise being present, the better you will get at it. When you've practised it a number of times you may notice that there's a typical pattern of distraction for you. Maybe you tend to check out of your body and feel disembodied. Perhaps you get lost in fantasy. Whatever it is, simply notice it.

SLOW DOWN, YOU MOVE TOO FAST

We've looked at the problems of fast-forwarding. In fact, our whole culture tells us that we should do more, do it faster, do it now – not just in sex but in everything we do. In sex the opposite is more often true. Instead of speeding up, we benefit from slowing down.

> *By slowing down and being present with each moment, we open ourselves to deeper layers of potential pleasure and a greater capacity for 'real sex'.*

Slowing down is also usually the exact opposite of what we see in most pornography. Pornographic sex limits our awareness and pleasure to the most reductive and simple level. It gives us the message that fast, hard sex is good. Fast sex has a certain type of energy that can feel delicious on some occasions but, overall, slowing things down leads to much deeper and more 'real sex'.

Pornography tends to focus on orgasm – usually the man's – as the goal of sex. Whether the perceived goal is orgasm or penetration, as soon as you start having sex with a goal in mind, you're not in the moment and this means you're not present. Sometimes there's nothing wrong with this type of focused sex, but if sex were always like this it would become just as stale as predictable sex in a long-term relationship. As we've seen, not being present takes us out of connection with our own felt experience and out of connection with our partner.

•••

It's a strange contradiction that while many people spend a huge amount of their time thinking about sex, when they are in a sexual experience most of them rush towards orgasm, as though they cannot wait to stop feeling the sexual energy in their system. This isn't because these people aren't enjoying sex, but because they feel unable to hold greater amounts of sexual energy.

Imagine a person's sexual energy is like water and that the person has a container to hold it. The container can only hold so much energy. Once it's full, any extra energy will spill over and can't be contained. Most people have only a very small container for their sexual energy. If the energy they hold becomes more than they are used to, they may feel that it's too much and start to edit it or discharge it by having fast sex or, as is usually the case in men, by releasing the energy through orgasm and ejaculation.

Part of the process of learning to have more meaningful and 'real sex' is to increase the size of your container. Size matters – but not the way you learned it did from pornography! Have you noticed how you feel as you begin to allow more sexual energy into your system without rushing to discharge it? Again, by being present with what is there in each moment you can become aware of subtler sensations.

Imagine blowing up a balloon. If we fill it with just a few breaths, there will be a small pop when it bursts. However, if we fill the balloon to capacity before bursting it, there will be a satisfyingly large bang since more pressure and tension has built up in the balloon.

The same is true of orgasm. The faster we reach orgasm, the less intense and satisfying it will be. By slowing down, we give ourselves the possibility of increasing the erotic tension and this will feel even more pleasurable when it's released.

Building sexual energy slowly over time not only gives us more intense pleasure but also creates a heightened sense of anticipation.

The longer gratification is delayed, the better
it feels when we finally let ourselves go.

Long, slow periods of bodily caress and foreplay build erotic tension. Focusing on the whole body moves the energy away from the genitals and creates a fully integrated experience of pleasure. Slowing down touch on the genitals themselves allows us to increase the erotic energy there before we let ourselves discharge it. Slowing down not only increases the amount of erotic energy we're holding in our system but also gives us awareness of new and subtler levels of sexual feelings.

INCREASE YOUR SENSITIVITY

If we have hard, fast, 'pornographic' sex, we'll likely miss the subtler cues of the body and keep our sexual experience only at a superficial level.

By slowing down sex, we give ourselves space and
time to feel a much richer, deeper palate of subtle
sensations and feelings that otherwise get lost.

Exercise: The *Karezza* – a Victorian Exercise in Erotic Mindfulness *(40 minutes)*

This exercise is a variation on the original version, developed by Dr Alice Stockham and described in her 1896 book *Karezza: Ethics of Marriage*. Its aim is to increase awareness of subtler sensations and to move away from orgasm as the goal of sex. The name comes, she said, from the Italian for caress – *carezza*.

This exercise is most effective with a partner but you can also do it on your own. It focuses on male-female partnering but includes other possibilities.

1. Start with the man lying on one side and the woman on her back. The man manoeuvres himself so that one leg lies over the woman's legs. The man brings his genitals into contact with the woman's genitals – it's important that they're touching. The man does not need to be erect although if he gets an erection during this process, that's okay, too.

2. If done between same-sex partners, either gender can simply hold their genitals against the other's and begin the exercise as above.

3. If you don't have a partner, you can simply lie comfortably and hold your hand over your genitals without moving it and without trying to make anything happen.

4. The idea is simply to lie with genitals touching, without movement, without penetration, for at least 30 minutes. Let your breath be soft and relaxed, breathing deeply without forcing it.

5. As you lie together you can make eye contact. Keep your attention in your genitals and notice what you feel as you lie together in this way. There may be a strong impulse to move into penetration. You may want to begin giving your genitals more stimulation. Resist the temptation to do so.

6. Maybe at first sight this seems like a stupid exercise and you may not notice anything happening. If you are used to intense stimulation or firm movements in penetration you might not notice the subtler feelings that can arise from this exercise.

7. Stay present with the experience and try to feel the subtler sensation of sexual energy – the background pleasure that is always available to us if we allow it and if we're not focused on how we expect sex to feel or look like.

8. After a while, you may begin to feel some gentle sensations first in your genitals then moving out through your whole body.

9. Allow this expression of Eros energy to flow through your body just by focusing your intention on sensation, however subtle or strong it might feel. Gradually it may begin to feel like a kind of sexual electricity shivering through your body.

10. It may be difficult to notice when you first try this exercise, but repeated practise of this exercise will give you intense feelings of pleasure and a deep sense of connection with your partner.

11. It's possible in the *Karezza* to experience orgasm without any physical stimulation or movement and for pleasure to flow through both partners without involving any sexual 'techniques'.

A TRULY SHARED EXPERIENCE

The deep and subtle sensations of sexual energy in your body that you can feel during exercises such as the one above are not limited to what you can feel in your own body.

The *Karezza* moves us away from the friction-based sex of pornography – friction where we rub two things together hard and fast enough until one of them explodes.

The Karezza *invites a deeper understanding of sexual energy and how profoundly pleasurable it can be.*

As you become more familiar with the *Karezza* exercise, you'll begin to feel a different type of sexual energy – less in the physical body and more at the subtle and energetic levels. Instead of intensity focused purely on the genitals, we can begin to feel tremblings – shivers of pleasure that spread through and enliven the whole body.

Once you begin to feel the energy moving in your own body, it's also possible to start to feel energies moving between you and your partner. You may notice that when your partner becomes aroused, you feel something happening in your own body – not direct stimulation but a subtler, more gentle type of arousal. There's a knowledge that what you are experiencing is not your own pleasure but your partner's.

It's possible to reach a point where you can even feel your partner's orgasmic response during sex. Once you've developed your sensitivity to the current of sexual energy flowing in your own system and you begin to feel your partner's energy in a similar way, you will be able to tell when your partner is orgasming even without any of the other obvious signals.

Your partner's sexual pleasure will be felt in your body and this will increase your own sensation and pleasure.

If both you and your partner are equally sensitive, a positive cycle is created between the two of you so that you can use both your own and your partner's pleasure to stimulate and deepen the pleasure you feel between you.

MASCULINE AND FEMININE ENERGIES

There's a difference in the way masculine and feminine energies yearn to be experienced. We open ourselves to these if we're able to feel the subtler energies that exercises like the *Karezza* can get us in touch with. When we speak about masculine and feminine, we don't refer to gender – that is, male and female – but to a deeper type of energy that flows in sex. The feminine energy seems to yearn to be seen. The superficial level of this feminine expression is dressing to look sexually appealing or to be noticed. By being seen, the feminine awakens desire in the masculine. This, again, is the staple of the majority of pornography. Women in porn are mostly there to arouse men's pleasure. They are often seen as objects for triggering male desire. By being seen, the feminine evokes sexual energy in the masculine.

The masculine energy, meanwhile, has a very different quality, yearning to awaken desire in the feminine by being sensed or felt. Men who dress flamboyantly are often described as looking more 'feminine', for example. While this doesn't mean that men shouldn't take care of their appearance, it isn't their presentation that tends to attract the feminine. It's the quality of their energy, their ability to be present, to which the feminine is most deeply attracted.

The difference in dynamics creates a harmonious circle of energy between masculine and feminine.

The feminine awakens the masculine through being seen, the masculine awakens the feminine through being felt. The masculine's ability to see the feminine is reflected in his presence. The greater the masculine's ability to be present, the more he can see the feminine and the more deeply felt he is, which in turn awakens the desire in the feminine.

As you open more to the subtle energies of sex, the more deeply you can sense and feel one another. This is the advantage of slowing down and opening your awareness to the subtler energies that can be felt in sex. When we move away from the raw, unrefined energy of pornographic sex and towards the subtler electrical energies that can be felt, we allow a deepening of the connection between ourselves and our partner. Sex increasingly becomes a co-created experience.

We feel not only our own pleasure, but also that of our partner and are able to use that sensitivity to help boost pleasure for both.

This deeper connection is also something that is felt. It does not arise from the mind or from thinking about it. It comes because we allow ourselves to focus on what 'is' – on our sensations, our emotions and the subtler energies that we feel in our body and in our partner's, rather than getting lost in technique or in expectations of what we feel should happen in sex. When we fast-forward or come into our heads we lose that essential connection with ourselves and with each other. Being present is one of the key steps to improving your sexual life and having 'real sex'.

THE CHALLENGE OF REAL INTIMACY

Real, authentic, deep sex that we've just described is a very intimate experience. The last, but usually most significant, obstacle to it happening is that we're longing for it but we're also terrified by it. Yes, most of us want great sex, but are we really prepared to be deeply intimate with ourselves, let alone intimate with someone else?

As we've discussed, to be fully in our body means that we have to face the reasons why we're usually out of connection with it: our shame, fears and insecurities. To avoid this, we've learned to stay out of connection with our bodies, which means, ultimately, out of connection with both ourselves and others – when we're uncomfortable in ourselves, it can be terrifying to be seen by others.

We all know the feeling of being 'talked at' by someone who makes no space for us. Most likely they are this busy talking because they are afraid of feeling themselves and, especially, of letting themselves be seen by us – so they cover themselves in a wall of words. It's the same in sex: if we're busy 'doing' sex, we're very likely uncomfortable with being with ourselves and, as a natural result, uncomfortable with being with others and being seen by them.

Foreplay plays a very important role in this yet it's one of the more complex aspects of sex. This is because it doesn't have any rules. It's like the pause in a conversation that can feel awkward because it leaves us 'naked' to feel each other, uncovered by the shield of the conversation.

In foreplay, we're feeling each other, we're feeling into, 'Are we going to have sex or not?', 'How are you feeling me; how am I feeling you?', 'What turns you on? What turns me on?' – in short, 'How am I feeling myself? How am I feeling you?' We are still within the sensual energy that we described in the chapter 'Understand Your Desire' (see page 49), which means the sexual energy has not taken over yet. Foreplay and the sensual energy don't have the same kind of mould.

Foreplay is very emotionally open, because we're feeling into each other and because we're wanting to connect. It's the moment when we appreciate each other and express our 'Yes' to the other – the opening to someone. This makes us vulnerable, for two reasons in particular. First of all we might be uncomfortable with expressing our emotions in general, as we just mentioned. Secondly, deep down we might not want to open to our partner, either because there are some unresolved emotional issues in the relationship, or because we're with someone we don't know well enough yet or with whom we don't want an emotional connection.

We're most likely to rush through the foreplay because we're avoiding intimacy.

As soon as we rush into the sexual act we're 'home safe' because sex, especially penetration, has its well-known routines. The 'conversation' continues, the openness between us is filled with activity and we feel less emotionally naked. And because sex has been modelled to us through porn, no matter if we've actively engaged in it or not, it has primed our understanding of what sex is, or is supposed to, look like. We have no collective image bank on sensuality and foreplay, so we have no other priming to fall back on. We haven't 'learned' to do foreplay; no one has taught us that this is important.

This makes us even more exposed. We are already in our bodies, in the sensual energy, feeling everything that is going on inside, and on top of that we're relating freestyle to someone else by being fully present. This can be too emotionally challenging and we might therefore tend to rush into penetration or a more direct sexual act because it's often less intimate. Unless you are in the fortunate situation where the sexual charge is so high that you feel compelled to get straight into genital contact, missing out foreplay is one of the biggest obstacles to great sex.

For women, who are generally turned on by touch and presence (as described in the chapter 'The Pros and Cons of Pornography', see page 23), foreplay greatly impacts their level of arousal.

Foreplay gives our nervous system a chance to relax and to allow our natural arousal to emerge, which greatly enhances our ability to experience pleasure.

If our yardstick is the felt experience of pleasure and connection – and not how 'right' it looks according to porn standards – great sex in general starts with good, long foreplay. This demands of us the ability and willingness to be intimate with each other, to say 'Yes' to ourselves and to each other fully, whether that is just in the moment or as an emotional, relational commitment.

It's also important, especially with a new partner, that we've negotiated our boundaries. If we haven't communicated clearly what we want and what we don't want, we're likely to spend the foreplay in a mental space of anxiety, out of our bodies and out of connection with our partner. So before having sex with anyone, ask yourself, *What level of intimacy do I want with this person? How much of myself am I prepared to show? How present do I want to be?* The answer will be a direct indicator of how deep you can go in the sexual experience, no matter whether it's a one-off or with a regular lover. It always takes place in the here and now.

KEY 5:
AUTHENTIC
COMMUNICATION

Great sex requires great, authentic communication. If there's one reason in our practice we consistently see people's sexual relationships going wrong, it's how they communicate with one another. Authentic communication requires courage, but the results are well worth it and it's one of the cornerstones of 'real sex'.

In our culture, we've never learned to talk about sex. The luckiest of us may have had the birds-and-the-bees conversation with our parents and some sex education at school, but this will most likely have been with a clinical approach with a view to avoiding pregnancy and sexually transmitted infections, never with information about pleasure and boundaries – how to make sure we enjoy sex.

Many will have had their first fumbling explorations of sexuality as teenagers, in their parents' house, with the possibility of discovery at any moment. Meaning any noise or talking during sex might have been heard. We came into our sexuality with the feeling that it wasn't really okay to be sexual, and for many young women, especially, it was definitely not okay to enjoy it and to want it.

If you feel as though you're not really allowed to have sex, you'll probably find it difficult to talk about it.

However, talking about it with our partner forces us to acknowledge that we're having sex and to take ownership of it. Authentic communication empowers us to make sure our partner knows where our pleasure is and what needs to happen in order for us to have our desires and needs met. Sadly, too few of us understood this as we learned about sex, so we ended up with miscommunication, withdrawal from intimacy and with dissatisfaction that is severely damaging for an enjoyable sex life.

Communication in sex, then, becomes something that either we assume is happening silently or we dare not broach. A code of silence envelops our sexuality through shame, fear, insecurity – or simply through ignorance. There's the magical idea that our partner, even a new partner, will somehow mysteriously know our desires and how we like to be touched. However, it's often hard for us to know our desires ourselves, let alone expect someone else to know and satisfy them.

It's not just when our partner is doing something we're not enjoying that we dare not speak our truth. It's also when we want sex that we keep quiet and hope the other will pick up on unspoken hints.

We may fear initiating sex because of
we've a fear of rejection or of being seen
as pushy – as 'sluts' or 'predators'.

In some cases, we may feel that what we're asking for is too much, that our partner would judge us if we really asked for what we wanted.

Straight, monogamous women, in particular, are not culturally primed and encouraged to own their sexuality and to actively want sex. In their fear of being judged as sluts, they'll either suppress their sexual desires and consequently become unfulfilled and resentful, or automatically reject sexual invitations because they feel they mustn't allow themselves to feel desire, which makes them equally resentful. This silent dissatisfaction of women who can't allow themselves to own and express their sexuality is toxic in long-term relationships.

Equally, when women don't own their sexual desires, men are forced into being the initiator and into learning that a woman's unspoken 'No' doesn't always mean 'No'. Sometimes she wants it but can't allow it to be expressed, which is why she's waiting for him to take initiative. This can be exhausting and confusing for men. It often leaves them with a projected 'dirty sexuality', making them a predator, and this is also a recipe for crossing boundaries. When we remain silent instead of communicating clearly what we want and what we don't want, we create confusion, unfulfilled sexual desires and a lack of boundaries.

> *A lack of clarity about our boundaries is one of the*
> *most frequent areas where people have problems*
> *with sex, and communication is vital here.*

Pornography has significantly influenced our perception of boundaries in sex. In porn movies it appears everyone is always up for everything, without any discussion; communication and dialogue are rarely the strong points of a porn movie. In reality, of course, everything is discussed in advance and what each player will do is already defined and agreed.

Too many clients have shared with us harrowing stories of the distress caused when their boundaries have, unintentionally, been crossed – and not just as teenagers. A prime example is when a woman keeps quiet about not wanting penetration and allows a man inside her. Another is when a person checks out of their body and dissociates themselves from it, losing contact with their bodily sensations – they most often do this owing to trauma or where certain emotions were not 'safe' or permitted in childhood, including sexual desire. They then find something is happening that they didn't want, but feel they've gone too far to say 'No', so they just close down and detach from the experience or allow it while freezing in fear or panic. Then there's the situation when a kiss becomes an uninvited caress and so on.

Yet boundaries are crossed all the time in sex, with people finding themselves doing things they didn't want to.

Even in a loving, safe relationship we may often find ourselves doing things to please the other, out of a sense of duty or obligation, that we don't truly wish to do.

Here, too, we're allowing our boundaries to be crossed. Once we've experienced our boundaries being overstepped, we're likely to carry the effects with us into other experiences, sexual or otherwise, either as a fear that makes us closed off and defensive or as an expectation of the nature of sex that makes our boundaries wobbly. How sex is 'supposed' to look and feel can affect our whole relationship with sexuality, often for decades.

SEX AND SILENCE

Sometimes people have their boundaries crossed intentionally, by abuse or in traumatic experiences. Far more frequent, though, are the times when our boundaries are crossed through silence, through not communicating what's okay for us and what isn't. We are often too embarrassed to say 'No' or 'Stop'. So how can we change this? How can we ensure that we create a sense of clarity both around our boundaries and our desires that ensures not only that we're safe, but also that we have the type of experiences we truly long for?

Sex, at least with others, is a complex and delicate social interaction. However, unlike other types of engagements, the normal rules of social behaviour seem not to apply. Think of it this way: if someone stands on your foot on the bus, you're likely either to move your foot or ask them to move theirs. On the whole, most people have a reasonable sense of what they are willing to put up with and what they would find unacceptable. If we feel our boundaries are crossed – that is, if we find something unacceptable – we tend either to remove ourselves from the situation or ask the other to change it.

In sex we typically find a different situation. One partner does something we don't enjoy and we often find ourselves thinking either 'I don't like that but I don't want to hurt their feelings so I'd better not say anything' or 'I'm not enjoying this but that must mean there's something wrong with me so I'd better not say anything.' We can even check out of the situation by disconnecting from our body and coming into our heads or check out of our bodies completely. To remove ourselves from the sexual experience seems rude or awkward, and since most people don't even know what they want sexually, they find it hard to ask for it, let alone to ask someone to stop doing something they probably imagine you're enjoying. It all gets very complicated very fast, so most people just stay quiet and neither complain nor ask for anything different.

This is a complete disaster, at least sexually speaking, and often at the more fundamental level of our personal boundaries. As we've already seen, leaving our body and coming into our head is a great way not to be present in sex and we've already seen the pitfalls of this strategy. When we do this, not only do we lose connection with the other and with ourselves but we're also no longer able to determine whether or not our boundaries have been crossed.

Silence starts as a small thing: a single action or sexual request that we don't enjoy but overlook. Compliance creates dissatisfaction but we hold our tongue. We don't wish to offend or disappoint. Very often our need to please is greater than our need to speak our truth. Our need for security may override our need for our personal boundaries. It's this silence that's the greatest killer of 'real sex'.

> *Silence is the cancer of sex; an insidious disease that causes so many sexual relationships to die out or break down into a gridlock of non-expression.*

In the beginning of a relationship we're so focused on the positive, the desire to make a good impression and on the enthusiasm of those first meetings, that we overlook what doesn't work for us sexually with this person and override our own needs or desires and the niggles and doubts that plague us about the sexual partnership.

Our fear of being 'too much' stops us from asking for what we truly desire so we settle for the safe options. Our fear of rejection, of being laughed at or of feeling shame is at the heart of this silence. Slowly and, of course, silently, the cancer grows. Another action is left unchallenged or not commented upon. Over time we find ourselves reduced sexually to what is a thoroughly unsatisfying, or even negative, sexual life and unsurprisingly our appetite for sex wanes. How could it not under these conditions?

OBJECTIFIER AND OBJECTIFIED

Our need to be the perfect partner – to please the other or to edit out our own needs and desires – creates a further disconnect from them. If our purpose is only to meet our partner's needs, we're allowing ourselves to be objectified. At some level our partner is no longer able to relate to us as the person we are but sees us as a means of reaching their own pleasure potential.

It's all too easy to be caught up in this desire to please. Pornography exacerbates this, especially for women, by showing us endless images of women whose sole purpose seems to be to act as objects of the man's desire, there only to provide pleasure and to be used, with – or seemingly without – their consent.

If we allow ourselves for just one moment to participate in a sexual act we don't enjoy, simply to please the other, we're diminishing ourselves and our sense of self-worth.

To do so is an act of self-abuse, no matter how small. The antidote to this objectification is to maintain a sense of self-worth that requires us to be treated as a person, not an object. This means not engaging in sexual (or, for that matter, other) activities where we don't feel acknowledged, honoured and respected for who we are as a person. During our work as sex therapists, we've noted that those who have the lowest sense of self-worth are those most likely to allow themselves to be subjected to the most negative forms of sexual experiences.

•••

It's worth noting at this point that in BDSM (Bondage-Discipline/ Domination-Submission/Sadism-Masochism) there can be the treating of oneself or the other as an object, but this is a complex and subtle role-play and, if performed healthily and consciously, not actual objectification.

One of the best ways to maintain this sense of self-worth is to learn to communicate your desires and your boundaries.

The better your ability to communicate, the better and more 'real' the sex you're going to have.

To maintain and develop this sense of self-worth we need to be able to speak our truth, to communicate our desires and our boundaries in ways that will be heard and understood. The only way through this wall of silence is to speak the unspeakable.

In order to feel safe, we need to have clear boundaries. Boundaries begin with oneself. We need to know internally what our own boundaries are before we can clearly communicate them to others, because we don't know how the other will behave or what the situation will bring up. Hopefully by now you've already been working with the nature of your desires and what they mean for you. If you've done the exercises as you've progressed through the book, you should begin to have some sense of what gives you pleasure and why you want it.

We need to trust our own boundaries and our
ability to put them up at any moment.

We can hone those skills by developing our ability to give feedback. By staying present in the moment, we concede that we may not know in advance what we want next but can feel and stay connected to ourselves. Just breathing into your body and asking yourself, *What am I feeling at this moment?* helps enormously. Ask yourself which 'mini-character' you're playing. For example, *Am I in the Performer? Am I in the Pleaser? What do I desire at this moment and that moment?* And so on.

SUCCESSFUL COMMUNICATION

Authentic communication falls into three parts. The first is knowing what you actually desire and where your boundaries are. The second is to communicate this internal landscape to your partner. The third is to do this in a way that's going to be effective.

If we alienate our partner with our choice of words, we're unlikely to get what we want. Understand that what you say, especially during or about sex, can impact the other very deeply. If we tell them, 'I hate it when you do this to me,' they are likely to feel rejected, humiliated, shamed or worthless and will most likely withdraw from intimacy. Such delicate interactions therefore require us to learn a new way of communicating. The basis of this is mutual respect. In order to communicate clearly and in a way that is respectful of the other, it's essential that we see both ourselves and our partner as people, with their own wants, needs, desires and vulnerabilities. This is the 'relational dynamic' and it's the core of good communication.

Exercise: The Yes-No Game *(60 minutes)*

This is a classic exercise from most tantra training schools that's very useful for helping you to understand your boundaries and to communicate them clearly without the other taking it to heart. You'll need to work with a partner, but it doesn't necessarily have to be one with whom you are intimate. You can perform this exercise fully clothed, naked or anywhere in between. Make sure you read through all the instruction points before beginning the exercise.

1. One of you is going to be the Initiator and the other is the Active Recipient. Decide who is who and position yourself comfortably sitting opposite each other.

2. The Initiator starts moving towards some kind of physical contact with the Active Recipient, but pauses before completing the move.

3. If the Active Recipient feels comfortable with this suggested touch in that moment, they will simply say 'Yes'. If they don't feel comfortable with that touch, they will respond by saying 'No'. If the Active Recipient is unsure, they can buy themselves some time by saying 'Wait'. If the Active Recipient would really like the Initiator to touch them in the way offered, if they feel enthusiastic about that type of touch, the Active Recipient will say 'More'.

4. If you are the Initiator, be true to yourself: offer the type of touch you would like to offer – but check with the Active Recipient before you give it. The idea of the game is to be playful and curious. Try to vary your touch and notice the different ways your partner responds. See if you can get each type of response from them.

5. As an Active Recipient, offer a response every few seconds or every time the touch varies in any way. Initiator, don't take your partner's responses personally. This is not about the touch that you offer but about the Active Recipient's individual response to it.

6. Play the game for about 10 minutes, thank each other for the curiosity and openness, and debrief the experience.

7. Active Recipient, how did you feel about saying 'No'? Was it easy or not? Did it come out angrily or were you afraid of offending your partner or of making them feel rejected? If you were able to give a clear 'No' several times, did you feel empowered? How did it feel to say 'Yes'? Were you able to admit that you were okay with certain types of touch? Could you let your partner know that you actually wanted 'More' sometimes? How did it feel to communicate that?

8. Initiator, did you allow yourself to suggest a kind of touch you wanted to make, or did you hold back for fear of overstepping boundaries, being judged or rejected? How was it for you to receive a 'No'? Were you able to stay aware that this wasn't a 'No' to you personally but to a specific kind of touch?

This exercise is useful in many ways. It can be used to learn what the other enjoys and what they don't. It's also a very powerful but simple way of helping someone to become more comfortable with saying 'Yes' and 'No'. In our clinic we often say that we love it when we hear a person's 'No'. This is because in intimacy we're so often guessing what the other does and doesn't like. In the worst-case scenario, if a person doesn't say 'No', it's possible to cross their boundaries in a very harmful way, even if we don't intend to. In most cases, however, it simply means that the person we're intimate with won't have a good time and this makes it less likely that they will come back for more, whether they are a regular partner or a casual encounter.

Hearing a person's 'No' stops us from having to guess what they want and lets us know what feels right for them at that moment – it's important to remember that their response is just a reflection of what feels right for them at that moment. All too often someone in a couple says 'No' to something and the other takes that as a blanket 'No', so they never try that thing again.

***Unless the person clearly says so, 'No'
doesn't mean they never want you
to try that thing at another time.***

It may mean they'd like to try it a different way next time.

It's also a great relief in our practice to meet someone who can say 'More'. When we offer intimate touch, we're always guessing what the person wants. Until we get a clear sign of their response, we continue to guess, and regardless of our sexual prowess or how good our intuition, at some point we're going to get it wrong – but not if the person always keeps us in the picture.

As we've mentioned before, most women have not learned to own their sexuality, which, to their partners, makes them seem like especially complex creatures. Their body may give non-verbal cues that have conflicting messages of 'Yes', 'No' and 'Maybe' at the same time. This makes it very difficult for the partner to know a woman's true response and can frequently create more performance pressure on them because they are trying to anticipate their partner's needs or desires. So, ladies, you can do your partners a huge favour by making any of these responses clearly, or by asking for what you want. When you do this, you take away uncertainty and doubt, you reduce performance anxiety and you allow the other to relax more into being present with you, knowing that, if something does not feel good for you, you will quietly and confidently let them know and they can change what they are doing.

This is all part of taking responsibility for your sexual self and your pleasure. The more we can be transparent and real in our sexual experiences, the more we help create a mutual sense of safety and trust in the sexual dynamic and the more all involved can relax into the moment and surrender to their pleasure more deeply.

Exercise: The Empress (or Emperor) and Slave Game
(60 minutes in each role)

This playful game explores some role-play to help you learn to communicate your desires more clearly. In the game, one of you will be the Empress or Emperor (we'll use Empress in this example) and the other is your Slave, there to do your bidding. You can do this with a friend or a lover. Make sure you read the instructions before beginning the game, and agree on a timeframe.

1. One of you assumes the role of the Empress and the other the role of the Slave, whose role is to pleasure the Empress. Of course, the Slave may have some boundaries, so if the Empress asks him or her to do something that he/she does not feel acceptable, the Slave may simply say, 'I am sorry, Empress, that is not within my boundaries to perform.'

2. As Empress you can ask for whatever you desire. It may be physical touch or it may be for your Slave to make you a cup of tea, read you a story or sing to you. You may desire your Slave to brush your hair or give you a back massage, or something more intimate.

3. The object of the game is for the Empress to continually keep feeling into herself and to ask herself the question, 'What do I desire in this moment?' In each moment your wish may change. When it does, let your Slave know and ask him or her to perform your new wish. Some desires may feel fulfilled after a few moments; others you may want to enjoy for longer.

4. There's no way for the Empress to get this wrong. Whatever desire you express is absolutely okay, even if it's not within the powers or the boundaries of your Slave to perform it. Each of your desires is beautiful: whatever your desire, at its centre is a core quality that is wonderful.

5. The joy of this structure is that you are playing a game – each person is role-playing someone else (although, of course, these aspects are

all really aspects of ourselves). This sense of playfulness and role-playing can be the gateway that allows us to cross over into giving ourselves permission to express our desires more clearly. Use this game as an opportunity to explore and express some things that you wouldn't normally ask for, and see what happens.

6. As Empress, keep asking yourself what would give you the most pleasure at this moment. How could you get your Slave to make it even more enjoyable for you? Notice what you edit out of your desires. What would you like, but don't feel confident or comfortable enough to ask for?

7. Empress, when the time is up, make sure you thank you loving Slave, then debrief the exercise, focusing on what you learned about yourself. If you are still feeling playful, swap roles.

In Step 6, what made it hard for you to ask for what you wanted? What resistances did you have to speaking your desires out loud? Very often it's because we think they are too much to ask or we judge them as 'dirty' or 'wrong'. We may simply not know what our desire is. Each of us has different blocks that make it feel challenging to ask for what we really want – but these can be overcome.

Helen's Story

Helen had been in a loving relationship with her girlfriend for the past five years. Although they loved one another and were physically affectionate, with plenty of cuddles and hugs, sexually Helen felt completely dissatisfied. The way that her partner touched her just didn't work for her. Helen found her touch too rough and she was too quick to dive towards the genitals. Helen was confused: she loved her partner and was physically attracted to her but couldn't really get turned on in sex.

It became clear from our work that Helen didn't really know what type of touch she enjoyed receiving. She was good at giving pleasure but not

*so good at receiving it. We began by teaching her to explore this with
her partner in an exercise we'll describe in the chapter 'Pleasure, Not
Performance'. By using this exercise, Helen began to understand what
type of touch she enjoyed. She was then ready to tackle the next big block
– communicating this to her partner.*

*Helen really struggled to ask for what she wanted. There was always
a voice in her head that told her that her partner would feel it was too
much. It turned out that Helen took a lot longer to orgasm than her
partner and because of this she felt inadequate and embarrassed. She
feared that if she asked for what she really needed to help her orgasm,
her partner would get bored and annoyed with her and walk out. So for
years she had settled for unsatisfying sex.*

*We worked on Helen's sense of self-worth and helped her to understand
that she deserved to ask for what she wanted. Through using the
'Empress and Slave Game' earlier, Helen could embody a new part of
herself and ask for what she wanted without feeling embarrassed.*

*At first she found it challenging. Naming her desires out loud felt
uncomfortable for her. To her surprise (but not to ours), her partner was
supportive and actually enjoyed helping Helen to have more pleasure.
She found it exciting that Helen was finally stepping into her sexual
potency and asking for what she wanted. It turned out that, all along,
her partner had also been feeling unfulfilled because she felt that Helen
was holding back, not really allowing herself to go into her pleasure. She
had interpreted the situation as meaning Helen wasn't as into her as
she had hoped.*

*This is a great example of how silence creates miscommunication and
distance between partners. In reality, Helen was very excited by her partner
and simply felt she couldn't ask for what she wanted. Helen's partner was
equally excited by Helen's pleasure and the more Helen accessed it by
asking for what she wanted, the more excited her partner became.*

*Helen had learned to speak the unspeakable. She had broken the silence
around her sex life and benefitted greatly from that. She learned that she*

had a right to her own pleasure and it was her right to ask for it. In her case, she had a very loving and supportive partner who was excited by the new parts of Helen she had seen in the game.

. . . .

So how do we ask for what we want in a way that is most likely to get the positive outcome we desire? The key to this is maintaining an awareness that the other has their own triggers and vulnerabilities and their own emotional responses to our needs. Remember that we can only have sex up to the level of our psychological development. This means that when we ask for something new it may be beyond our partner's (or our own) comfort zone. Judgment arises when we're at the edge of that zone. It's in those places, where we feel uncertain or insecure, that we're most likely to judge ourselves and others. If our desire is met with judgment, this doesn't mean that it's wrong, simply that our partner has reached a growth edge within themselves. Asking for something new, then, is a beautiful opportunity to expand and develop. Framing the judgment not as 'what I want is wrong', but as a learning opportunity, can help us to have a new experience.

Exercise: Being Asked for Something Challenging
(30 minutes)

What would it mean to you if your partner asked you for something that you didn't feel comfortable with? You might instantly rush to judgment or resistance, but here we invite you to look again at your own reaction and see what's really going on. Keep a notebook and pen close to hand and write down your insights as you go along.

I. Imagine that your partner comes to you and says they would like to try something new sexually that you would find challenging. It might be a new sexual position, role-play or a scenario involving others.

Reading this, you might already have an example from your real-life experience or you might want to imagine something that you know would be challenging.

2. When you have something in mind that you know would challenge you, in your mind's eye create as vivid an image of the situation as you can. See yourself having this conversation with your partner and feel into how that would be for you.

3. Take a moment to breathe into your body and notice what emotions are here for you. Are you feeling ashamed, awkward, angry, jealous, disgusted or judgmental?

4. What is the deeper reason for your emotional reaction? What does it mean to you for your partner to have this desire? Do you think it means you're not enough for them? Or are you afraid of feeling awkward or insecure?

5. Can you find the part of yourself, the 'mini-character', that is triggered by this idea? How old does that part feel? Is it a child part? Does it evoke emotions that you experienced earlier in your life – from your childhood, perhaps? Try to get as clear a sense as possible of the part of you that is feeling challenged.

6. When you have a clear sense, dialogue with it: ask it what is really bothering it. What is the fear really about and what would it need to feel loved and secure? Listen – and take your time.

7. When you've heard everything this part has to say, in your mind's eye imagine yourself giving it everything it needs. If it's hugs and reassurance, give them. If it's a loving friend by its side, imagine this. If it's confidence, dream it up. Just visualize this part of you being happy, loved and at ease.

Our judgments always arise out of some kind of fear, and the antidote is to feel loved and secure. This is very good to remember, both when we're the one feeling judged and when we judge the other. When we invite someone out of their comfort zone they will have their own fears and insecurities activated and they will need to feel loved and secure. Always be compassionate and gentle when you put out a wish for change. Know that your partner's potential resistance is arising out of fear and insecurity, as your resistance is within you.

> *Always encourage your partner. Help them to understand that while they are already doing a good job, there are some things they could do that would give you even more pleasure.*

For example, try saying something like this: 'I love it when you touch me there, but it would feel even better if you slowed down and touched other parts of my body before we focused on that part. In that way I get even more aroused and can enjoy your touch even more.' Or you might say, 'This feels good but it would feel even more yummy if you pressed a bit more gently.'

Such language is simple but effective. It does not shame the person giving you the touch. In fact, it affirms them while at the same time making it clear what you want. Very often this approach is effective, as the partner feels that what they are doing is good already, so their ego isn't dented by this feedback. They then learn something new about what you like. If they are treating you like a person and not an object, they will listen to your lovingly offered comments and try to take this into account.

Another powerful tool for authentic communication is learning to speak from the deeper place of your core quality rather than from your superficial desire or want. For example, we may want our partner to slow down in sex, not to rush into penetration or ignore foreplay. This is our desire.

By applying the model we described for 'mini-characters', we can understand that our behaviour and our wants or desires are simply covering a deeper need for something else.

That need might be safety, contact, pleasure or another thing. Within that deeper need is the core quality – perhaps the quality of connection, empowerment, ease. When we communicate our wishes from a place of connection to this deeper need we're far more likely to be heard.

What does this look like? If we want our partner to slow down in sex and we examine why we desire this, we may find, for example, that it's actually because we want to connect more deeply with them rather than just rush into penetration. If so, we might try communicating this as well as our need for the outer behaviour to look different. Instead of saying, 'Don't just rush to having full sex. Slow down,' we might try saying, 'I'd really love to feel more connected with you and when you rush into penetration I can't feel as deeply connected to you as I'd like to.'

By communicating this we let our partner know our deeper intention, which as a core quality always comes from a positive place rather than arising out of fear. We're able to communicate our deeper yearnings and give an explanation of why we want something to be different rather than simply telling them they're wrong.

Speaking from the place of our deep needs and core qualities also allows our partner to see the deeper longing in us and gives them an opportunity to meet us there.

This also helps you to avoid getting sidetracked by unhelpful discussions about who is right and who is wrong.

If at first they don't seem to respond to your invitation to be different with you, you can let them know how this makes you feel. 'When I ask you for something different and you ignore me, it makes me feel like you don't love or respect me, and that makes me feel less like having sex with you.' By using such language you are simply stating your experience. This isn't a threat to withdraw sex, it's just an observation of how their behaviour impacts you and how that affects your desire for intimacy with them. It's important not to get into making threats unless you are willing to carry them out. For example, if you say, 'Unless you touch me differently, I won't have sex with you,' then they fail to change their touch and you go ahead and have sex with them again, you've just invalidated your position; you've lost your bargaining power. They know that your threats are idle and they can simply continue doing what they were doing without any consequences.

If your partner doesn't listen to what you are asking for, you may need to stop what's happening. This doesn't mean blackmailing your partner, forcing them to grant you any desire if they want to avoid your threat of withholding sex. However, if you're making reasonable requests that are consistently ignored, you may eventually need to let your partner know that you have certain needs, and that while you want to be intimate with them, this only works if you are enjoying it, too. So, until they are ready to listen to what you want, so that both of you can enjoy the experience, you may have to limit how much access you give them to your body.

Exercise: Say What You Mean *(As many minutes as you need for lovemaking)*

This is an exercise to try when you feel more confident with your partner. You should only try this when both people in the dynamic are able to take responsibility for themselves and know that whatever comes up for them in the process comes from their own issues, and is not the fault of the other. It's also important to know that whatever judgment or quality we project onto the other is always an unowned aspect of ourselves. If this feels too much, you can start by doing this exercise through self-pleasuring.

1. In this process we invite you to have sex or make love with your partner and say out loud whatever thoughts come into your head at each moment. Both partners do the same simultaneously.

2. The idea is not to listen to what the other says but to notice your own thoughts and mental imagery and to bring these into awareness by describing them. These thoughts might include awareness of pleasure or of less pleasurable sensations. You may be bored or uncomfortable in a certain position. You may move into fantasy and away from the actual physical experience. It might be that you begin having thoughts about another person or wishing that you were doing something else sexually in that moment. Just speak them all.

3. Notice how you feel as you let yourself speak your thoughts and desires. What do you edit out and what do you allow? If you perform this exercise several times with the same partner, you will probably notice that you become more willing to speak your thoughts and desires each time you do it and that it becomes easier.

4. When you find a thought that you would like to suppress, mentally make a note of it and come back to it afterwards. Then you can do the mini-character visualization from earlier in the book to discover which part of you wants to express this desire and which deeper need would be met in expressing it. What is the core quality you would get in touch with if that part were to be fully expressed?

5. After the session has ended, make sure you take some proper time to debrief the experience with your partner, both of you reflecting on what is usually unspoken in sex and why that is. Make sure you are gentle and loving with each other, and that you speak from your heart with a mutual desire to learn about yourselves and each other, and to grow together.

WORKING WITH FANTASY

One of the areas that can be most challenging when communicating with your partner is naming your fantasies. We can easily get caught in the idea that, 'That isn't allowed' or 'I would feel ashamed if I told them about this fantasy that I have.' But you might be surprised by what fantasy your partner finds sexy, and even challenging bits can be turned into a wonderful breath of fresh air in your lovemaking.

But here's an important point: if you have a fantasy, it's not about the particular person or scenario within it, but what it represents to you: the way you are longing to experience yourself. It represents a part of your sexual self that is a longing for expression; a part that makes this particular experience so charged for you.

> *Very often we use our fantasies to live out aspects of ourselves that we're not yet prepared to fully own.*

These are likely to be our most sexually charged, vital and potent expressions, the ones we usually edit out in our actual lovemaking because social conditioning tells us that it wouldn't be alright to be this sexual. Fantasies, then, hold some important core qualities for our sexual expression. It's not the act itself that counts but what you make it mean – and remember that everything you experience in fantasy can be put back into regular lovemaking with your partner.

Another crucial point is this: by including, integrating and communicating your fantasies with your partner, there's something to be expressed that is of benefit to both of you. The more you own and communicate how you are longing to feel sexually, the more of your authentic sexual self you will bring to the encounter and the more of yourself there will be for your partner to enjoy.

> *If you are at the receiving end, remember that your partner's fantasies are never a threat – they are an opportunity to enrich your sex life.*

When we hold back, our partner will hold back, so neither of us is fully present and our sex becomes limited and limiting.

So we would suggest a maxim at the heart of every authentic communication: 'Hear without fear.' Our resistance to our partner's fantasies, and even our relationship with our own fantasies, can almost always be reduced to some kind of fear. As in the 'Being Asked for Something Challenging' exercise (see page 161), if we dig deeper than our immediate response of 'that would just be weird/disgusting/too much', we'll find our judgments often arise out of some kind of insecurity and fear that has nothing to do with the actual situation. If we can hear our partner vulnerably share their longing to connect with their deepest desires as a desire, too, to connect with us at a deeper level, and to have more pleasure with us, we create the opportunity to allow more intimacy and to grow together.

At a practical level, to begin working with fantasy it can be a great idea and great fun to write down your fantasy. You don't have to be a Booker Prize nominee to do this. You are only doing it for your own pleasure, so just enjoy it. Writing your fantasy is a very playful way of giving yourself permission to have it. This doesn't mean you need to act out your fantasies.

Many fantasies are pleasurable only in fantasy and we would never wish to act them out.

But you might like to explore some fantasies in reality. As long as you're safe, relating to others as subjects, not objects, and you're not putting yourself in danger, that's a choice for you.

As we've seen, sexual shame is one of the biggest inhibitors to pleasurable, 'real sex', and when we can divest ourselves of these feelings we liberate ourselves not only sexually, but also in every other area of our life, too. Exploring our fantasies is a very powerful way of shame-busting. By writing down our fantasies, we allow ourselves to let go of the power they may have to shame us. In fact, when we write and explore our fantasies they very often lose the charge they hold over us. If we're fixated on one particular type of fantasy, writing it and saying it can be an excellent way of letting go of the energy we've been keeping stored up around it. When we free up this energy, we can use it for different fantasies or other activities, sexual or otherwise.

Spend some time writing down all the details of your fantasy. Really allow your mind to be creative and to focus on both the physical acts and appearance of the scenario, and on the sensations and emotions behind the fantasy. Let yourself imagine how it would feel to live out this fantasy. Don't hold back from using language that would turn you on. This is just an exercise in expressing yourself; it doesn't become any more real or likely to happen just because you've written it down.

Once you've spent some time writing your fantasy (and you may want to write it out several times to see if it changes or if you wish to refine it), then with your partner you can begin to name your fantasy. Remember that naming the fantasy does not mean it will happen or that you even want to make it happen.

Before you read out your fantasy, make sure your partner knows that the reason you are sharing it with them is because you want to bring more of yourself to your lovemaking and to experience more passion with them. Make sure your partner is able to 'hear without fear'! Then make an agreement with your partner that what you are sharing is a fantasy, nothing more. It's not a suggestion that the two of you make this happen in the real world. It doesn't show who you are sexually but it is a part of your sexual self, which as we've seen is a vast and wide-ranging collection of different aspects of yourself.

When we allow ourselves to explore our fantasies, we open up new aspects of our sexuality. The joy of fantasy is that it doesn't need to be something we truly wish to act out. In fantasy, everything is permitted. When we share these fantasies with another person we make these new parts of ourselves available to them and available to be loved. This can create a deeper bond between partners and open up new avenues of pleasure and sexual exploration in the relationship.

Another area where fantasies are generously indulged is in sexting and sex-positive online chat forums.

A lot of highly charged energy can be generated in these situations, very often because we're chatting to anonymous strangers or because we're texting people we either don't know very well yet or, obviously, are physically separated from. This distance creates a kind of 'safe zone' to express our more raw sexual desires without the vulnerability of personal, intimate connection; we know we're not really going do it, especially not right now. This can be a wonderful, enriching and very charged experience, but in terms of authentic communication it poses a challenge because it creates a blurred boundary between fantasy and reality. If we're chatting or texting people we're planning to meet up with, we've created an expectation that can be difficult to follow through. Either we go into performance anxiety or we feel we've 'promised too much'. In either case, we lose hold of our own boundaries and can potentially end up in situations where we compromise our personal safety.

If you enjoy sexting, chatting and fantasizing, that's wonderful. Reply to messages and exchange as much as you enjoy, but be clear that it's a fantasy. How far you want to take it in reality is a whole other game that needs its own boundaries to be discussed. If, by the time of the actual meeting, you still want sex, be clear when communicating your boundaries as to what is 'Yes', what is 'No' and what is 'Maybe' – and make sure the other party consents to that.

However much and at whatever level you decide to share your fantasies and desires, the key to 'real sex' is authentic communication. Breaking the silence around sex can feel like one of the hardest, most personally challenging things we can do. However, when we're able to do so in a loving and respectful way, it leads to huge personal growth in both our intimacy and many other areas of our lives. While the risk of breaking the silence may seem great, the benefits of authentic communication mean that we get to truly be ourselves in our sexual interactions. This is real intimacy – the type of intimacy that each of us longs for and that touches us deeply.

KEY 6:
GIVING PERMISSION

In order to allow ourselves to feel pleasure, we first need to give ourselves permission to experience it. This permission is fundamental to our ability to connect with pleasure. The idea of permission, particularly in the context of sexuality, seems closely linked to ideas of right and wrong – a kind of moralistic perspective that places sex and innocence as the antithesis of one another. As psychotherapists, however, our view is that sex itself is innocence and that, once more, society has its perspective on sexuality askew.

According to US online dictionary Merriam-Webster, innocence is the quality of 'freedom from guilt or sin'. It also uses the words 'blamelessness' and 'simplicity' to describe the quality of innocence. These latter qualities can prevail in an adult sexual situation as much as in childhood.

When it comes to sex, innocence isn't about what we do but about the feelings and judgments that underpin it.

Sex is a natural expression, not one that arises from social constructs. As mentioned earlier, we come from a billion-year-old lineage of sexually active antecedents. Having sex is in our genes, as well as being an evolutionary imperative. We are therefore blameless for our desires to have sex; sex and desire are natural impulses.

Of course, how we express these impulses, and with whom, can give rise to judgments, and it's from these judgments, not from acts and behaviours, that problems arise of the loss of innocence through sexual activity. Such judgments are social constructs – they are simply ideas, not a reality, unless we choose to substantiate them in our own lives. The loss of virginity, for example, is a prime case. What is a person's virginity? Most people would say that it's a quality that a person has before they have penetrative sex for the first time. Virginity is said to be lost when a woman's hymen is broken through the penetration of a penis. Does this mean, then, that lesbians remain virgins if they don't have sex with a man? The idea is clearly false. We might broaden the definition of what constitutes 'sex' and take it that when we begin to have sexual experiences with others – however we interpret that – we lose our virginity. Again this seems a limiting idea.

An alternative definition of virginity might be based not on what we've done physically, but on our own judgments around our actions.

If we allow that sexuality is more about the energy and intention then virginity, too, becomes more about these qualities than about the actions associated with them. Virginity, then, in a more meaningful sense, is linked to innocence. It's the state of 'purity' – not of action, but of intention. A child who explores their body or mutually explores their friends' bodies in innocent games of doctors and nurses is no less innocent or virginal for having done so. The loss of innocence or purity – those virginal qualities – arises from the feelings we may experience having done something sexual. We are taught by society that sex is not innocent, that at many levels it's something we should feel shame around.

It is shame that causes us to lose our innocence, not the sexual acts themselves.

In this way, someone who has had a negative sexual experience the first time around may, if they can reconnect with their innocence as the quality of purity of thoughts, feelings and judgments about sex, reclaim their virginity in terms of energy and emotion. When we relabel sex as innocence by reframing our understanding of these qualities, we can begin to understand sex from a new point of view and from this place begin more fully to give ourselves permission to allow sexual pleasure.

Sexual innocence is sex freed from the shame that arises out of culturally imposed judgment. And it's in sex freed from shame that our deeper pleasure is hidden.

OUR RIGHT TO PLEASURE

There's a strong argument for sexual pleasure to be a basic human right. It's a fundamental aspect of human sexuality and most of us would accept that it includes the right to choose with whom we share our sexuality and how we do it, without coercion, violence or discrimination based on gender or sexual orientation.

Shockingly, this is not a given, even in the Western world. Despite a brief expansion of freedom around sexuality in the mid and late 20th century, when Dr Alfred Kinsey's research[12, 13] and the *Hite Reports*[14, 15] were published, sexual pleasure hasn't been on the agenda with regard to human rights. The fact that it has re-emerged in recent years is at least in part owing to the gay rights and the feminist movements.

Even so, it seems a huge oversight not to include sexual pleasure in our human rights alongside our choice of partner.

Meanwhile, sexual pleasure remains a highly charged topic in most psychotherapy and biomedical fields.

A good measure of a society's maturity is to assess its relationship with sexual pleasure and permission; the more responsibly permissive the society, the more mature. Many societies' relationships with sexuality are both top-down and bottom-up constructs. At one level, the state controls what is sexually permissible. The most obvious example of this is homosexuality, which until 1967 was unlawful in the UK. Changes in legislation gave permission for gay men and women to enter into freer sexual relationships without fear of legal consequences.

From a bottom-up perspective, what the average person on the street feels about sex also influences our collective opinion of what is sexually acceptable. The things we see in the media, how we talk about sexuality with our friends, the type of images that are permissible on social media – all impact what we feel about sex and how much permission we can give ourselves to enjoy it.

Sadly, sexual pleasure as an essential human right is not widely acknowledged. Take the dispute that erupted in France in 2013 around the issue of whether or not disabled people have the right to work with sexual surrogates – trained professionals who help to guide a person through a series of processes, including sexual intimacy, in order to help them achieve their therapeutic goals regarding sexuality. Unable to readily find other sexual partners and feeling likely to be exploited by sex workers, many disabled people turned to surrogates. Surrogates are typically highly qualified, often with a master's degree in psychology or psychotherapy, and act in conjunction with a psychotherapist who oversees the therapeutic relationship between surrogate and client. This approach has become well known through the award-winning 2012 film, *The Sessions*.

Concluding its investigation into disabled people's right to use surrogates, the French National Ethics Committee declared, 'The sexuality of the disabled cannot be considered a right.' It seems that when we fight to give ourselves permission to experience pleasure, we're fighting not only our internal resistances, learned in family systems, schools, the media and so on, but also a collective denial of the right for sexual pleasure, from the top of society downwards.

In order to reclaim our essential right to pleasure, we must first give ourselves permission to have that pleasure. This arises not from the outside but from within. Society has the distorted perspective that sex is something that happens when we connect with others. We are told that we feel sexually aroused when we meet someone else, be it a romantic partner or a sexual playmate. The 'other' is the one that evokes our desire, our lust or arousal. So, often we wait passively for this special 'other' to appear, to arouse our desire, to make us orgasm, believing that until this happens we cannot access our sexual self. In fact, it's quite the opposite.

Sex starts with a relationship with oneself.

This is how, as children, we learn about our bodies and about sex if we're given the space, freedom and safety to do so. We innocently explore our bodies, discovering which parts feel good to touch and learning, over time, how we enjoy being touched on them. It's not uncommon for little girls and boys to begin to consciously explore their genitals for pleasure from the age of five or six years old. Some scientists suggest that, even in the womb, foetuses touch themselves for pleasure.

Young children do this simply because it feels good and they have, if raised sufficiently safely, a sense of curiosity about their bodies and the world. Once discovered, innocent self-exploration will usually continue until an adult intervenes and tells them that this is not okay or that they need to be careful about how and where they touch themselves like that. The child will then commonly feel shame about their behaviour and may either refrain from it or continue surreptitiously.

Again, loss of innocence arises not from the act itself or from within but from the judgments and feelings that we learn from others. It is imposed from the outside by parents, teachers, peers, religion, media and others. In order to reclaim our right to sexual pleasure, we need to give ourselves permission to reconnect with our sexual innocence.

We cannot truly begin to have a full and free sexual relationship with others until we have one with ourselves.

Your sexuality is not defined by anyone else unless you choose to allow it. Your sexuality is not something that's given to you by others. It's important, therefore, to begin by building up a sexual relationship with oneself. We covered elements of this in the earlier chapters 'Understand Your Desire' (see page 49) and 'Know your Sexual Self' (see page 75).

When we can create our own sense of our sexuality,
we no longer allow it to be defined from the outside.

We're also no longer reliant on others to give us permission to be sexual. The impulse to feel our sexual energy and to express ourselves sexually comes not from outside but from within us. We can begin to build up a sexual identity, a sense of who we are as sexual beings, irrespective of what is happening around us.

This sense of self is not dependent on whether we have a current sexual partner or not. It's not dependent on how many times we have sex or what type of sex we have. Even if we're having types of sex that we don't necessarily wish for, such as sex coming from a place of obligation or duty, sex that lacks fulfilment and satisfaction, we can still maintain a sense of our sexual identity within that is unaffected by external circumstances. We can, in effect, retain our innocence.

The idea of loss of innocence arises because of
the beliefs that we hold about sexuality.

Many such beliefs are learned from parents, from school, our culture and so on. In modern society, increasingly strong influences come not from those immediately close to us, but from the portrayal of sexuality by the media and in pornography. Men and women born in the 1980s and 1990s onwards have been increasingly subjected to distorted messages about sex that leave a negative imprint on their ideas about sexuality.

It's also possible that we may inherit beliefs and emotional 'residues' from previous generations and there is growing scientific evidence for this. If our family lineage has a history of sexual trauma or abuse, or a difficult relationship with sexuality, there's a school of thought that says these beliefs will be passed down through generations. Trauma has been scientifically demonstrated to be passed down generations of mice, for example.

Exercise: Dissolving Sexual Fears *(30 minutes)*

As we saw in the very first exercise of this book (Sexual Myths, see page 20), each of us has absorbed into our psyche and our system messages about sex that impact our relationship with it as adults. We fear that if we give ourselves permission to express our sexuality fully, there will be negative consequences. Even if, as adults, we don't believe in these messages anymore, their paradigm may still exist in our psyche. This exercise is a variation of the Sexual Myths exercise, and will help you understand how these messages have created sub-conscious fears of sexual self-expression".

1. You'll need some reflective time on your own, and your notebook and pen.

2. Start by casting your mind back to your childhood. When did you first hear about sex? How did you feel when you heard about it? Were your parents or carers sexual with one another? Or with others? How did that feel? What impact did sex (having it or not having it) have on their relationship? What else did you learn about sex?

3. Take a moment to reflect on this first imprint of sex and relationships. How did this impact your adult relationships? Are you repeating any patterns?

4. Below are listed some fears we have about expressing ourselves sexually. Take a moment to reflect on them. Which ones are familiar to you? And do you have some new ones to add?

If I give myself permission to fully express my sexuality, then:

- I'll be judged as being dirty/cheap/slutty

- No one will want me

- I'll be seen as 'too much'

- I'll feel ashamed

- My partner will abandon me

- Other people won't like me

- It should be for someone else, not me

- I'll lose control

- I might want it too much

- I'll be judged as selfish

- I won't be safe

- I'll be punished (in this life or the next)

- I'll be taken advantage of

- It'll hurt someone I care about

- I'll get a sexually transmitted disease

- I'll get pregnant

- I'll be letting someone down

- I'll be a bad boy/girl

- I'll bring shame on my family

5. As each of these messages arises in your awareness, notice how you feel in your body. Notice the link between the belief, the feeling and the bodily sensation.

6. As you notice each sensation, simply breathe into it, bringing your awareness to that part of your body. By doing so, you can create more space around the belief and begin to make room for it to dissolve.

7. Feel the belief melting away in your body as you are breathing into it, telling yourself that this is an old belief that's not true and doesn't serve you anymore.

8. You might want to tell yourself why it's not true and replace it with a new positive belief – an affirmation that embraces your sexuality in a supportive way.

9. Spend some time breathing into the positive message, receiving it with your mind as well as your body.

10. Imagine yourself as a conscious, loving, caring parent who teaches your inner young-adolescent child the positive, empowering messages about sexuality that you would have liked to receive. Give your inner child permission to develop into its own natural, beautiful, alive, vibrant, potent, full sexuality.

THREE TYPES OF PERMISSION

Permission is what can replace the old negative and limiting beliefs about sex. Permission is what empowers us to make clear and conscious choices about how we express our sexuality and with whom. In this we notice that there are three types of permission that it's essential to be able to give ourselves in sex.

1. Permission to Be a Sexual Being

We need to permit ourselves to have a sexual identity that we own for ourselves, without waiting for someone else to activate it or to approve of it. This is about becoming comfortable with our sexual self and our desires.

2. Permission to Allow Ourselves Pleasure – to Lose Control and to Express Our Wildness

Permission for pleasure has two different aspects. The first is 'Permission to Lose Control'. The fear of losing control is frequently linked to orgasm. Orgasm is a letting-go, a loss of control at some level. This can feel frightening for many people.

Orgasm is a moment of mindlessness, a moment of no thoughts and a temporary suspension of our sense of self.

In French this is called a mini-death – *la petite mort*. This is a terrifying prospect for most people. In its highest form this is a fear of annihilation, a fear that we'll somehow cease to be if we surrender to the power of our orgasmic bliss. There can be a feeling of emptiness and immensity with an intense orgasm that creates a connection with a vastness beyond oneself that is both thrilling and highly unsettling for the ego, our sense of self. It's this feeling of powerlessness that can prevent many people from experiencing their deepest orgasmic pleasure.

At a less existential level, you may also fear losing control of your bodily expression. If we fully surrender to orgasm, our body takes over with its own sounds and movements, which many people feel awkward about. In orgasm we can't 'keep up appearances', which can be hugely challenging for people who tend to have a certain controlled expression or who feel the need to be 'perfect'.

This touches on the other type of permission that we need to give ourselves for pleasure, which is the ability to express our wildness. Wildness might look very different from the way we usually present ourselves – which might be awkward for some, for the reasons just mentioned – but we might equally avoid expressing our wildness because we fear judgment of this more spontaneous and untamed part of us.

Very often we fear that if we fully express our sexuality, it will get 'out of hand', that we'll want more than our partner or more than society tells us is acceptable – society tends to judge and malign those who express their sexuality in a wild and passionate manner. We tend to feel shame, and possibly fear of rejection, if we access our unbridled sexual desires.

The fear of being seen as 'too much' is very common.

But instead of thinking of yourself as being over the top, perhaps it's more the case that others may not be enough. This reframing can take away the feelings of shame that arise when we truly want to express our fullness, especially in a sexual way.

Permission to Say 'No'

The final type of permission we need to give ourselves – one which is equally, if not more, important than the 'positive' expressions of sexuality – is to say 'No'. As we explored in the chapter 'Authentic Communication' (see page 147), trusting that we can say 'No' is key to our ability to be present in sex, to feel safe and to fully express our playfulness in sexuality. Saying 'No' to what we don't want is as important to enjoying our sexuality as it is to say 'Yes' to pleasure.

Saying 'No' creates clear boundaries, a feeling of safety and mutual respect that provides the frame in which our pleasure can unfold.

It allows us to let loose, be spontaneous, abandoned and playful without fearing that the experience would get 'out of hand' and we would then have to do something we didn't enjoy or want to do.

Saying 'No' from an empowered place is not a denial.

When we say 'No' to one type of experience we're actually saying 'Yes' to another one.

'I don't want quick, disconnected sex' (our 'No') could at the same time be a 'Yes' to a more connective, engaged and slower experience, for example. This links back to communication skills by ensuring that we communicate more authentically what we truly desire. Increasing our aptitude for authentic communication enhances our ability not only to say 'No', but also to move into our 'Yes' and ask for what we do want.

Denying ourselves these permissions leads to denying our sexuality, feeling less alive and less engaged with the world, and to increasing difficulty in having deep and intimate relationships. It stops us from allowing pleasure to be felt in our body and from creating a safe space in which love and intimacy can flourish. It seems essential, then, to our wellbeing, both sexual and otherwise, that we learn to give ourselves permission in each of these categories.

However, giving ourselves these permissions would mean taking responsibility for our sexuality and desires, and this might feel shameful.

Avoiding shame is a big payoff for denying ourselves such permissions.

After all, we can always blame others for our lack of sexual experience. We might tell ourselves, 'It's not my fault. No one asked me to be sexual with them,' or we might say, 'It's not my fault I have sex. I'm just doing what my partner wants.'

What's more, if we truly own our desires we might realize that we have a greater sexual appetite than we thought, perhaps a greater appetite than our partner believes they have or an appetite for other sexual partners. Owning our desires can have a destabilizing impact on a relationship, but the good news is that such destabilization is exactly what's required for relationships to evolve. Such challenges in a relationship are wonderful opportunities for both parties to grow, even if that involves the desire for different kinds of sexual expression with your partner – or with others. As we explained in the previous chapter, 'Authentic Communication' (see page 147), all desires can be brought back to this basic question: how are you longing to experience yourself? Communicated in a compassionate way, the answers can be a wonderful guide to growing in your relationship.

However, instead of facing these opportunities for growth in our relationships, we tend to shy away from them to avoid rocking the boat, and in doing so we keep ourselves small and limit our pleasure, our self-expression and our sense of self gradually becoming diminished. We feel less confident, less able to be free and, over time, we lose our aliveness and our capacity to engage with the world in a meaningful, intimate and enjoyable way.

INTERNAL JUDGMENT MAKES EXTERNAL MIRRORING

Not giving ourselves permission to own our desires also has a knock-on effect: we tend to judge what we don't accept within ourselves.

> *When we judge something in ourselves, we unconsciously send out signals to others that this part of us is not okay.*

This creates a judgment in others because they pick up on our own internal judgment and, unless they are highly attuned to their own perceptions, which most people are not, they will simply accept your judgment as their own. If we don't give ourselves permission to love and to accept our desires and our sexuality, we'll have a negative judgment about that. Since we hold this judgment, the energy with which we approach sexuality will have an unclear or unclean quality to it. Others will then pick up on this unclear quality and mirror it back to us. It may look like a sleazy, unaccepting or shameful quality, depending on the exact nature of our own relationship with it. In this way we create our own reality and affirm our negative beliefs through the way we experience others' reactions to us. When we judge ourselves, those negative beliefs will be reflected back from the outside.

We therefore unconsciously create a vicious circle for ourselves.

> *Our lack of permission to be sexual creates a reaction in others that in turn reinforces our negative self-image and beliefs.*

The more we wait for others to approve our sexuality, the less likely they are to affirm it in a positive way. The more we await that external approval, the more we give away our power to others. We give them the power to make us right or wrong; the power to tell us whether we're attractive or not; the power to give us permission to be sexual – or not. Our lack of ability to give ourselves permission is based on these old, limiting beliefs that arise mostly in childhood, beliefs you will most likely have encountered in the previous exercise.

It's from these beliefs that our internal self-judgments and self-criticisms arise. They arise when we move beyond our comfort zone and into a significant new area of understanding – our growth zone. The only question that matters is whether we'll step over the edge of our comfort zone or choose to revert to judgments based on those old beliefs.

Despite our fears, when we step beyond our own judgments something beautiful emerges. No matter what we may previously have thought about ourselves, if we can truly give ourselves permission to express this new emergent part, we'll find that it's loved and accepted by others – because other people will feel our own acceptance of it and make that self-acceptance their own perception of you. When we give ourselves permission, it follows that others will, too. A kind of space emerges within us when we stop judging ourselves. It's in this space that something new emerges. By giving yourself more space, more of you can emerge. And as more of you emerges, parts that have become split off or disowned can be reintegrated and you will grow and mature in richness and depth.

Internal permission, then, is what drives external permission – not the other way around.

When we give ourselves permission to be sexual, it is, essentially, an act of growing up. When we're children, we unconsciously absorb the beliefs and stories that we hear in the world around us – this thing is good, that one is bad and so on. We believe the messages our parents tell us, whether these are about sex or anything else. It's an act of growing up and of exerting our own independence and uniqueness in the world that makes us first question their authority, their truths and their beliefs. So with our sexuality, when we truly grow up, no matter what our age, we begin to challenge the limiting beliefs about sexuality that we learned as children and to reassess our own relationship with it from an informed, adult place rather than a reactive place where we either fight against parental (and societal) control or submit to it.

> ***The question is whether we want to take the risk of finding that adult place within ourselves or to stay in the safety of our limited, childhood beliefs around sex.***

When we're truly giving ourselves permission to be in touch with our sexual energy, we can feel it flowing through us like a life-force energy. We may feel it in our pelvis and genitals, in our heart or somewhere else in our body. Sexual Eros energy has a particular quality – a warm, pleasant, tingling sensation. It makes the skin and the body area you feel it in feel alive. This is our natural state of being, to feel this energy in us at any moment. It has nothing to do with whether we're going to express ourselves sexually or not; it's simply our aliveness and our life force pulsing through our bodies. Now, let's try to feel it.

Exercise: Connecting With Your Sexual Energy
(20 minutes)

This exercise will help you to connect with your sexual energy as it flows naturally through your body as life-force energy. It's not unusual not to feel anything the first few times you try it. This is to be expected. After all, you've trained yourself not to feel it due to all the reasons and stories we've described in this book. But the more you practise this exercise, the more you will feel the power of these pleasurable sensations in your body.

1. Make some quiet time and space for yourself where you won't be disturbed. Lie or sit in a comfortable position and make sure your spine is straight but relaxed.

2. Begin by bringing your awareness to your breath. There's no need to make the breath do anything in particular – simply bring your awareness to it. Do just this for several minutes until you begin to feel yourself fall deeper into the experience of your body.

3. As you begin to relax and soften, bring your awareness down into the larger area of your pelvis, your hips, your bottom, your anus and your genitals. Notice how you feel in that part of your body.

4. Now focus your awareness on your sacrum – the base of your spine, above your tailbone, the back of the girdle of the bones of the pelvis. Note that this is not directly near your genitals; yet it's where we can first feel our sexual energy.

5. Imagine that you can breathe into your sacrum. In your imagination, feel a tiny movement of the bones as you breathe into them, the subtlest of vibrations or movements of energy in that part of your body. If at first you don't feel it, imagine that you do. 'Fake it 'til you make it.'

6. As you continue to breathe into your sacrum, feel the warm, tingling sensation growing there. Let the feeling grow in intensity. Imagine that the tingling feeling is getting more and more pleasurable.

7. Allow the sensation to spread and increase. Imagine there is a colour associated with the feeling and that you are now turning up the 'volume' of the colour so that it becomes brighter, clearer and more intense. As you do so, notice the intensification of the sensation in your sacrum, too.

8. There's nothing you need to do with this energy – just let it be there and notice it. Notice how you feel as it comes into your awareness. Can you allow it or do you have a desire to edit it? Does it feel pleasurable and exciting or scary?

9. When the experience feels complete for you, gently bring yourself back and notice how you feel in your body. Know that you can tune in to this energy in your body at any moment of your day.

This exercise wasn't in any way aimed at sexual expression or the use of sexual imagery. However, if you can allow yourself, you are likely to begin to feel not only the pleasure of the tingling sensations in your pelvis, but also to notice a desire to link those sensations to sexual awareness – perhaps to desire, perhaps to fantasy or other sexual impulses. This is exactly what happens when we give ourselves permission to feel the natural flow of energy in our bodies without judgment or fear.

This flow of sensation is a normal, healthy and natural expression of your life force. Feeling it is proof of your aliveness. That aliveness also wants to express itself sexually.

Notice how innocent the quality of this energy if we don't label it as sexual.

It's no different from the impulse that makes kids climb trees or run about and play. It's only when we bring in judgments and labels about it that we become challenged by it. By calling it sexual, we bring into play all our learned ideas about why sex is bad or unsafe.

By returning to a natural state of innocence we can more readily give ourselves permission to feel that sexual energy and enjoy it for what it is: our aliveness.

Sexual energy is a naturally felt part of our bodily experience if we give ourselves permission to feel it. What's interesting, then, is how much we edit out of our awareness. Typically, when we begin to feel those physical sensations connected with our arousal we'll often edit them out. When we have sexual thoughts or desires, either in sex or in normal daily life, we'll often edit them out. So much of our desire is edited out, leaving us with only the leftovers to feel. This reduces our sexual life to a tiny part of its possible potential. We limit not only our desires and drives but also our pleasure and, ultimately, our capacity for intimacy with ourselves and others.

Exercise: What Do You Edit Out? *(Ongoing)*

In this exercise we're going to look at how you react when erotic feelings come up. At this stage you might already feel blocked by a voice that says, 'I don't have any erotic feelings.' Many who don't have an enjoyable sex life, especially women, will experience their libido decreasing to a point where they feel they could live quite happily without sex. However, since you are reading this book, this is unlikely to be entirely true. For various reasons, we might shut off our identity as sexual beings and unconsciously edit out sexual feelings, but that doesn't mean the sexual energy is absent. It will come up in our dreams, our cravings for food, clothes and gadgets, and often in numbing strategies such as alcohol, television or excessive cleaning.

If this all resonates with you, every time you feel a craving or the need to numb yourself, try playing with these ideas using this exercise. Be open to the possibility that your lack of sexual desire might come from an inner belief that your desires can't be met, for whatever reason in your life situation.

1. When you next notice some erotic feelings rising up in you, whether you're on your own or with another person, become aware of the voices in your head. Notice what you allow yourself to say or do and what you edit out.

2. Be aware of the subtle sensations of pleasure in your body and whether you can fully allow them or not. Notice if you have a desire, however small, fleeting and impulsive, that you don't fully express.

3. Notice the stories you come up with as excuses for not saying or doing what you want. Without making any of these voices 'wrong', just notice them.

4. It can be useful to do this exercise daily over, say, one month and write some notes at the end each day so that, over time, you can begin to build up a picture of what you allow and what you don't. Notice if there's a pattern around the stories you tell yourself that inhibit you from fully expressing your sexuality.

5. Do your stories have a theme? For example, are the things you edit out linked to your body image? To how others perceive you? Are they connected to moral judgments about sex or something different?

6. When you begin to have a clear sense of the themes of the voices blocking your sexual energy from fully expressing itself, go back to the first exercise in this chapter, 'Dissolving Sexual Fears' (see page 177), and compare the two lists against one another. Is there a connection between the two? Can you see how the messages you received about sex as a child could be linked with how you limit your sexual expression as an adult? Is there a connection between what your parents believed about sex and how freely you give yourself permission to express your sexuality?

EMOTIONAL TOLERANCE

As we grow into more mature human beings, we tend to increase our capacity to be okay with a wider range of feelings – including our desires. This is our 'emotional tolerance' – our ability to allow ourselves to feel more intense emotions. At the bottom line, this is the purpose of any therapy. Therapy helps people to allow themselves to feel the sadness, grief, rage, loss, love or longings that they've previously blocked because feeling these was too uncomfortable. The therapeutic process helps people to lose their fear of these emotions and supports them in feeling what was unfelt before.

Very often when people consider this, the assumption is that if feelings are uncomfortable they must be 'negative' or dark ones such as fear, anger or sadness. However, as much as we block out this type of feeling, we also tend to block out more 'positive' emotions such as love, joy, excitement, spontaneity – as well as desire and pleasure. Childhood experiences where these feelings weren't welcomed now limit our capacity to have such pleasurable emotions, and we treat these 'good' feelings as though they are 'bad'.

This kind of ambiguous emotion is very likely to produce shame.

As we develop our emotional tolerance – to any type of feeling – we learn to cope with the ambiguous feeling where pleasure and shame are combined. We develop our capacity to step out of our comfort zone and embrace new ways of expressing ourselves. This means we also increase our ability to feel more and more pleasurable sensations. Our range of sexual desires will also increase as we grow and we'll give ourselves permission to enjoy different types of sexual pleasure or experiences.

Society tells us that sex within a loving, monogamous relationship is the only type of sex that is really acceptable. In fact, it's expected of us: it fulfils the obligations of the relationship. Society also tells us that certain sexual acts, with certain people, are permissible and others less so.

As we grow our ability to tolerate ambiguous emotions, we can increasingly give ourselves permission to expand our sexual repertoire and possible partners.

Once we've built our 'emotional tolerance' to allow pleasure for the sake of pleasure, we can more readily allow sex for the sake of sex.

We no longer need to limit it to an agenda for our relationship or as a way of meeting a need for external affirmation. In other words, sex becomes about doing what we feel like from a place of joy and pleasure rather than being driven by our 'shadow motivations' – the reasons for our actions that arise out of fear, not love.

Equally important is our capacity to say 'No'. In committed relationships there can be a strong impulse, or even pressure, to say 'Yes' to sex when we don't truly want it. Often, we do this out of a sense of duty or guilt, or because we don't feel good enough or worthy enough to decline. As we discussed earlier, these are all shadow motivations for having sex. We have the right to feel sexual but equally we have the right *not* to feel sexual. We have the right to choose our sexual partners and we also have the right to choose the type of sex we have with those partners. This means that if your partner wants to have a particular type of sex and you don't want that type of sex, you have a right to say 'No' and a right to say 'Yes' by asking for the kind of sex you do want. As we saw in Jane's story in the chapter 'Understand Your Desire' (see page 49), it can be easy to mistake a lack of desire for one type of sex (penetration only, for example) with a total loss of desire ('I don't enjoy sex').

> *When we say 'No' to the types of sex we don't enjoy, we create space for a different type of experience to emerge, which might include types of sex that you do want.*

Increasing our emotional tolerance builds self-confidence and, in turn, this grows our ability to say 'No'. Think of it this way: if you feel under pressure in your relationship to have sex, look at the shadow motivations for this. Perhaps it's because you're afraid that if you don't have sex your partner will reject you or go elsewhere to have their sexual needs met. Maybe you feel that your partner will simply not like you if you don't have sex with them. Of course these may be considerations that need to be taken into account and discussed with your partner, but it comes down to a shadow motivation – having sex out of fear of the consequences of not doing so rather than engaging from a place of pleasure and desire.

The shadow motivation is driven by fear of a feeling that we don't wish to experience. For example, your story might be, 'If I don't have sex, my partner will reject me.' The more we can tolerate the discomfort of facing the fear of rejection, the less we'll be governed by that fear. Perhaps we'll be rejected, perhaps we won't. In a sense, the fear of rejection is less important than how we feel about the experience of being with those emotions.

> *If we can face our fear of rejection, it*
> *ceases to have power over us.*

We can then act from a place of our own impulses rather than being ruled by fear. Of course, this is a difficult place to get to and maybe none of us fully achieves complete emotional tolerance. However, the less we live in fear of our feelings, the more we're able to say 'No' and the more we're able to embrace pleasure.

> *If we sufficiently develop our 'emotional tolerance',*
> *we can express our sexual selves fully.*

Fear will no longer be the driving force that either compels us to do things we don't desire, or blocks us from expressing our natural sexual impulses.

It's important, too, that not only do we give ourselves permission to be our true sexual selves, but also that we allow ourselves to be seen as such. Some people can allow themselves permission for a wide range of sexual expression in privacy but could not allow those parts of themselves – those 'mini-characters' – to be witnessed by others. For as long as we do this, we continue to separate out and compartmentalize different aspects of our sexuality and in doing so we don't fully give ourselves permission to be who we truly are.

Part of being seen as a sexual being is not only what we do but also how we appear to the world. Perhaps you can let yourself be seen as a sexual being on your own or with a partner – but can you also allow this in a wider, more public setting? Again, our sexuality does not arise simply when we're in relationship or when another wakes it up for us. Our sexuality is an inherent part of our very being: our essence and our life force.

> *If we limit our sexuality to what is allowed when we're in relationship or to what our partner permits us to express, then we limit our sense of self and allow it to be defined by others.*

The way we move, how we dress, what and how we eat, how we express ourselves verbally and the movements of our body are all elements of our sexual self, whether we're in a relationship or not, and all give clues as to whether we truly own our sexuality or not. If we don't have language for our intimate body parts (breasts, penis, vagina, anus and so on), we most likely don't have a good healthy relationship with them – or with ourselves.

When we talk about owning our sexuality and fully expressing it, that doesn't necessarily mean being sexual with everyone we have a desire for. And of course we need to respect the boundaries of our relationships and others' right to say 'No' as well as our own right. But when you give yourself permission to express your sexuality, you can fully own it, you can take full responsibility for it without waiting for others to shape it for you or to give you permission.

> *Your sexuality belongs to you, it is yours and it is a wonderful part of you.*

You have a right to express it consciously, self-lovingly and fully, in whatever way is appropriate for you.

KEY 7:
PLEASURE,
NOT PERFORMANCE

At the start of this book we shared with you the story of Jenny, our client who wanted to be taught how to give an amazing handjob. In her therapy, Jenny did not specifically get what she asked for. She went away with something much more valuable. She realized that learning some advanced techniques to give pleasure would not in fact lead to greater heights of better sex for either her or her partners. In fact, she recognized that her desire to perform what she hoped to be fantastic sexual techniques was actually what was stopping her from having great 'real sex'.

Performance is so often a distraction from the main experience of being sexual. It creates a tendency to 'do' sex rather than just 'have' it and enjoy it.

> ***Performance is what happens when***
> ***we don't have a strong relationship***
> ***with our own pleasure.***

Performance can so easily become the default, go-to option that leads not to greater sex but to pressure and anxiety – things that kill desire, not enhance it.

Pornography, of course, is pure performance. As discussed in the chapter 'The Pros and Cons of Pornography' (see page 23), actors in a porn movie are just that – actors, performing for the camera and for their audience. They're just 'doing' sex, not 'having' it. What they do, how they look, how they move, the sounds they make are all part of that performance. It's easy to be seduced by the feeling that we need to look a certain way to be sexy, that we need the perfect body or that we need to 'do' sex in a certain way in order to be good at it.

However, sex isn't about the 'doing'; rather, it's much more about the 'being'. The impulse to perform in sex arises from earlier, childhood experiences, very often nonsexual. If we have a tendency (and most of us do) to feel that how we perform in bed is important, this will probably have been reinforced by the media and, especially, in pornography. Articles in glossy magazines tell us about '51 ways to pleasure your man' or how to have the 'best orgasm ever'.

Imagery and ideas sold in such publications promote the misleading idea that if you learn some fancy techniques, you too will be able to have great sex.

The truth is that such techniques are by their nature a thing of the mind. They are intellectually defined constructs that require us to think about what we're doing. This requires us to be in our heads. We've already examined the perils of coming into our heads in sex. We may tend to fast-forward, skipping ahead if only by a few seconds to what we think ought to happen next; this may be something we are afraid will happen.

All sorts of funny thoughts and ideas come to people while having sex – some people genuinely make shopping lists – but many more are caught in the performance trap. And the more they feel they have to perform, the more they come into their heads, and the more they are in their heads the less present they are with themselves and with their partners.

Here are some thoughts that clients have told us come into their heads during sex:

- Is he/she enjoying this?

- Do I look good from this angle?

- Am I doing it right?

- Am I good enough?

- Can he/she see my scar/fat/bald patch/saggy bits?

- Is he/she bored?

- Why isn't he/she more turned on?

Some of these thoughts may seem quite amusing when expressed aloud, but for the people who have them they can be crippling. All these thoughts share the idea that there's a right way to be 'doing' sex and that if they don't get it right, perhaps even 'perfect', then there's something wrong with us.

So how and why do these thoughts arise in us and how can we change them?

> ***The key to shifting from performance to pleasure is to understand your own relationship with your pleasure.***

Before even looking at sexual pleasure, examine your relationship with pleasure in general. How much do you allow yourself to experience pleasure in your life? Can you enjoy a good meal or a glass of wine? Do you allow yourself to take time to enjoy nature or beauty, perhaps through the arts, if not from an intellectual perspective then as a felt sense. Similarly, can you give yourself permission to enjoy the feeling of your clothes on your body or of your nakedness? If you've done the exercises throughout this book you'll have begun to have a better sense of the pleasure your body can offer you without it needing to be sexual.

When exploring the idea of pleasure, it's important to understand that pleasure is a felt, embodied experience. There can be pleasure in intellectual dexterity or brilliance, but even this is felt as a sensation in the body, perhaps as a glowing feeling in the chest or a warmness in the abdomen.

Pleasure is essentially of the body. This is the fundamental reason that it can be so difficult to allow.

To be 'in our pleasure' requires us to be 'in our body'. Even if we allow ourselves some pleasure, it's all too common to remain an observer, staying in our heads to distance ourselves from the felt experience. We may feel that this keeps us safe – safe from the feelings of shame or guilt that we may feel in relation to our own pleasure.

As we've discussed, particularly in the chapter 'Know Your Sexual Self' (see page 75), shame is a huge deterrent both to sexual permission and to pleasure. It may be that we were shamed as children when we began, innocently, to explore our own body's pleasure. Maybe we were shamed when we were caught with our hands in the cookie jar, wanting more than the permitted amount of pleasure.

Perhaps there's a link, at least in Western culture, to Christianity. When people think of Jesus Christ, the image that tends to come up is that of Christ on the cross. Christ, we're told, suffered for us, for our sins. Suffering is essentially linked to the Christ figure. Perhaps, then, suffering is seen as noble and virtuous, and pleasure as a 'sin'. Even if we don't hold this Christian perspective, its influences in our culture are deep and operate at an unconscious level in most people of Western background.

PLEASURE AND EXISTENCE

This deep and often painful question invites us to look at our beliefs about pleasure and our own existence. Was pleasure and playfulness allowed in your childhood? How was your spontaneity received in childhood? Were you 'too loud' in expressing yourself? When you expressed your creativity, was that encouraged or were you told you shouldn't do that or that your attempts at creativity weren't good enough? Many of us learn at school that we need to express ourselves creatively in specific ways. The 'right' means of artistic expression are prescribed by conventional norms and rules that are often in conflict with our own inner drives and creative nature. Alternative and free-thinking ways of self-expression are not generally encouraged. When we learn to draw, as children we're often told that we should do so in a particular way. The same goes for learning music and most of the arts.

So the small child's impulse to cover themselves or the walls of their bedroom in paint is discouraged. Perhaps they are told their desire to express themselves freely by rolling around in the mud is wrong – mum has to do the washing, after all. We are told to be a good boy or girl and to behave nicely. We learn not to speak our truth but to anticipate what the grown-ups around us expects us to say.

> *We seek to avoid disapproval – from our parents, from teachers and so on. We stop taking risks because we fear rejection or being shamed.*

We fear that parental love will be withdrawn if we're not 'good' children. We may feel that we're worthless if we don't behave in a certain way. To avoid such feelings, we learn to limit our pleasure and our creative expression.

> *Gradually we learn that freedom of expression is not okay, that we need to learn to behave and to be civilized human beings, not display our raw, wild expressiveness.*

Over time, our childhood exuberance dims. Our pleasures become more and more limited until we find that the palette of our pleasure is reduced to nothing more than drops. Once we allow our pleasure to be taken from us, it's not long before our very aliveness feels crushed. To express our pleasure goes against our childhood programming – what we learned about our worth, our right to express ourselves freely, our very right to exist. Look at the average 40-year-old on the street. He or she will tend not to have the same aliveness that we can see in the eyes of children.

We must ask ourselves, do we deserve pleasure? Is pleasure something that's permitted and are we worthy of it? Since pleasure is about embodiment, about being in our bodies, on this Earth, we can also say that ultimately pleasure is linked to our right to be alive. It is, we can argue, an existential question.

Do we have a right to enjoy being alive?
 Do we have a right, even, to exist?

At the deepest level, the question of pleasure asks us: were we welcomed into the world and did we feel safe within it?

Take the example of the playful child kicking around in the mud. They have no responsibility; there's no accountability for their actions. If their clothes get dirty, an adult washes them. When they want clean clothes the next day, they go to the chest of drawers and, magically, there are clean clothes. This is how it should be for a child. Their environment is cared for and their needs met. However, as we grow we increasingly take on more responsibility. At some point we start having to wash our own clothes, at another point perhaps we take on a mortgage. Little by little the burdens of responsibility grow and correspondingly the permission we give ourselves for pleasure diminishes.

Ideally, in childhood we're carefree and able to express ourselves freely without needing to have too much concern for our environment. We should be free to explore, to express and to enjoy without worrying about whether our mum or dad is going to become too upset. We're not talking about a boundary-free idyll where a child's destructive behaviour has no consequences, but one in which there's room for playfulness and where a child's natural curiosity and desire to explore the world for their pleasure is allowed.

> ***Too often, though, we learn as children that***
> ***we're responsible not only for ourselves***
> ***but also for those around us.***

If a parent has a temper or a predisposition to anger or violence – whether against us or the other parent – we'll likely learn to suppress our joy. We'll likely learn to keep quiet and small and to hide our emotions lest we attract the wrong sort of attention. If a parent suffers from depression or anxiety, we'll learn to play the pleaser, showing only positive emotions in order to try to keep them happy and stop them getting into dark moods. There's no room for other feelings such as our own sadness, fear or anger.

In each of these cases we adopt a specific strategy that is later likely to inhibit our ability to experience pleasure; our awareness is 'out there' on the other. To avoid Dad's rages we learn to read his mood and steer clear of him when he's angry in order to stay safe. To stop Mum falling into depression (a child will very often feel it's their responsibility to keep a parent happy in such cases) we learn to feel when she is on the edge of her sadness and make an extra effort to buoy up her mood by seeming to be jolly.

It's as though we have an internal radar that is constantly checking for other people's moods so we can avoid feeling unsafe. We learn to anticipate when to avoid people or when to behave in a certain way. We learn what other people want and can get very good at meeting other people's needs. This is, of course, a great gift. It's the gift of empathy – being able to feel and sense what is going on for others. Many such people later become carers or nurses. They are also common in the therapeutic profession because they've learned to read other people so well. If you are in a caring profession, you might like to ask yourself if any of this rings true for you.

Such empaths also make wonderful life partners because of their ability to meet their partner's needs. However, this strategy only works up to a point.

You might be wondering what's wrong with having such wonderful sensitivity to others, with being unselfish, supporting your partner or helping them meet their needs?

The downside of this particular gift is that our attention is almost always 'out there', on the other. In focusing so much of our awareness on the other, we often lose connection with ourselves.

YOUR EMOTIONAL CENTRE OF GRAVITY

Imagine your awareness is a ball of energy, perhaps a small, glowing golden ball. Think of this as a visual metaphor called the 'emotional centre of gravity'. You could imagine this ball of energy sitting somewhere inside your body, perhaps in your abdomen or maybe in your chest. When you're on your own, the awareness is, ideally, within yourself. You can sense how your body feels, what impulses and desires are there for you and what thoughts and feelings you are having.

Now imagine that someone enters the room you're in. Your awareness suddenly shifts onto the newcomer. Your emotional centre of gravity moves out of yourself and onto them. This isn't a bad thing: it's important to assess if the new person is a friend or a threat. We need to understand what they want and if we're safe. This is a healthy shift of our awareness. If someone were to explain this concept to you verbally, face to face, part of their awareness would be on you, to ensure that you understood what they are saying. They would want to know whether your facial expression registers understanding or confusion, for example, so they could know whether they had described this idea to you successfully.

Now, if their emotional centre of gravity were balanced, they would be able to have part of their awareness on your experience

(*Does he/she get what I'm saying or not?*) and part on themselves. They would be able to regulate their own experience while simultaneously assessing where you are in it all. This is a healthy expression of our emotional centre of gravity.

If, on the other hand, the majority of their awareness were out there on you, they are likely to lose connection with themselves and will only be able to feel you. In doing so, they are likely to forget where their boundaries lie and to have them crossed. They are more likely to meet the other's (your) needs and make their own needs less important or even forget them completely.

In sex, we are also likely to focus our awareness on the other's experience, to attend to their pleasure and ignore our own.

> *While being generous in sex can be fun for both parties, if this is your habitual way of being, either in a relationship or in sex, it will tend ultimately to be destructive and unsatisfying for both parties.*

Jim's Story

In his mid-forties, Jim earned very good money, had an impressive address, drove a sports car and had recently started a relationship with 'the most beautiful woman I have ever met'. Over the years, Jim had had a string of fabulous-looking women, he'd enjoyed a playboy lifestyle and had been very active sexually. From the outside, his life appeared to be a textbook success.

However, in the bedroom he wasn't so lucky. He found that while in casual encounters he'd had no problems maintaining his erection, but now that he was in his first emotional relationship his potency was suffering. He was also suffering from early ejaculation. Visits to medical professionals had provided him with a ready supply of Viagra, but even on the pills he still had problems with maintaining his erection and when he did get one he peaked far too soon.

As we began to work, it became clear that Jim had two main focuses for his attention in sex. The first was on his genitals. Were they going to perform? Was he hard enough? Could he last long enough? The second was on his partner. Was she enjoying it? Would she be critical? Did she seem satisfied? What did she want? His attention was so much on her and her judgments that he couldn't tell where his own pleasure lay.

The focus of our work with Jim was to encourage him to spread his attention away from his genitals and his need for them to do things in a certain way, and to bring his awareness back to himself, regaining a more focused emotional centre of gravity. We encouraged him to focus on the moment, not to get lost in expectation of what he thought should happen next. By slowing down to focus on his whole body, he was quickly able to feel more of his body and to enjoy more sensations of pleasure throughout the body, not only in his genitals. Jim tentatively began to reduce the dosage of Viagra and found that while his attention was diverted onto the rest of his body, his genitals were actually doing what he wanted them to.

Over the course of three months, Jim was able to come off the pills completely and rely on his own sensations to give him pleasure.

He was also able to maintain his erection. His early ejaculation went away, along with his erectile problems. For Jim, his problem wasn't solved by medication but by simply shifting his emotional centre of gravity and becoming aware of his whole body during sex. Taking the pressure off his genitals to perform allowed him to relax enough that his normal, healthy arousal could come and go without him failing into anxiety and stress over it.

At first Jim was concerned that shifting his emotional centre of gravity away from his partner would make him seem selfish and make him a worse lover. In fact, the opposite happened. As he began to feel himself more, he was more able to be present with his partner and both of them enjoyed each other more.

• •

Exercise: Where Is Your Emotional Centre of Gravity?
(10 minutes then ongoing)

In connecting with others, we very often lose touch with ourselves. This exercise will help you bring the focus back to yourself so that you can be truly present and authentic in your connections. You can try this exercise with your sexual partner, with a family member or a friend. You can even try it with strangers in a social setting when you talk to a shop assistant or the waiter in a café.

1. In preparation for the exercise, you need to find your emotional centre of gravity. Find a place where you are alone, sit quietly and breathe into your body. Take your time.

2. When you're feeling relaxed and centred, imagine your emotional centre of gravity, that ball of light in the middle of your chest.

3. Take your time to feel it, see it in your mind's eye, breathe into it and familiarize yourself with the feeling. This is your point of connection to yourself, to which you can always return.

4. Staying in that knowing, you are now ready to move into the world and connect with others.

5. Now, when you next find yourself in connection with someone else, bring your awareness back to that imaginary ball of energy. Has it moved out onto the other or is it still within you?

6. If it's out there to some extent, where would you visualize it if you could see it? Is it closer to the other than it is to you, or is it, say, halfway between the two of you?

7. If the ball of energy is more than halfway away from you, imagine that you can rebalance this emotional centre of gravity. Bring it to a place about halfway between you and the other. Allow yourself to feel not only them but also yourself.

8. Practise this until you find what feels like a healthy balance point between you and them. Keep readjusting it as you go. Notice how it moves as the conversation progresses. Do you have a tendency to keep moving the ball of your awareness back towards them or can you hold it between the two of you?

This simple exercise can be profoundly life-changing if your awareness is habitually on the other. It's good to practise it in different circumstances, with friends, with your partner if you have one, in sex and in life in general. Get used to building up a greater awareness of your emotional centre of gravity and start to learn to manage it so you can exercise some control over where you place it. The greatest test of this is often in sex. Begin to practise bringing your awareness back to yourself in sexual situations so you can begin more strongly to feel your own body, your own desires and your own boundaries when you are in these situations..

Typically, if your emotional centre of gravity is out there on the other, you will go into 'performance' and not focus on your pleasure. For most people, performing for the other is to give them pleasure. For others, it might seem as though their awareness is on themselves, but when we examine it more closely it turns out this is only so they can focus on how they appear to the other. For these people, how they look in sex and how their partner perceives them is very important.

This preoccupation with the other's judgments and perceptions takes awareness away from us and brings it onto the other.

If you are the type of person who tends to constantly ask themselves questions such as *Do I look okay from this angle?* or *Can he see my wobbly bits?* then while your attention might be on yourself, ultimately your awareness is on the approval of the other, and hence on their pleasure and not your own.

It's possible to link this behaviour and many similar ones back to the important question we raised earlier in the book: why do you want to have sex, anyway? (Perhaps remind yourself with another look at the chapter 'Understand Your Desire', see page 49.) We asked, what's your motivation for having sex? Is it a golden motivation such as love, connection, pleasure and so on? Or is it more of a shadow motivation like the need for external approval or the feeling of obligation or doing what is expected of you?

> *If your motivations generally arise from a*
> *'shadow' point of view, then the likelihood is that*
> *you are not focused on your own pleasure.*

The key here is to understand whether you are having sex for yourself or for someone else. If it's for someone else, then you are going into performance of some kind – either the giving of pleasure or the performance in order to get your shadow needs met.

Here we can also tease out a difference between the type of sex that we might commonly have in a long-term relationship and more casual sex. In casual sex we're more likely to want to impress. We will tend to make an effort to look our best, use our best moves and to try to give the other some pleasure. In this we often get lost in the performance aspect of sex. How we look during sex or whether our partner has an orgasm or not might feel important. In fact, statistically, women are far less likely to have an orgasm on a one-night stand or with a new partner than they are when in a relationship. This could partly be because a relationship can create increased feelings of trust that more readily allow the woman to orgasm, or it may be because they are more concerned about performance and therefore less present in their body and with their experience.

In more settled relationships, the inhibitor of our sexual self-expression is something else. Whilst performance plays a part for many in relational sex, another force takes over from pleasure.

The drive for sex often arises from the needs of the relationship's agenda and not from the desire for pleasure.

We might tell ourselves, *We should have sex; it's been a while* or *I can't say no; if I don't have sex they'll find it elsewhere* and so on. Such agendas within relationships are shadow motivations for sex. When we get lost in the agenda like this, we tend to overlook our own pleasure. A different type of performance pressure kicks in, one that is based less, perhaps, on appearances and more on the need to perform for emotional reasons. Either way, performance is a massive pleasure-killer.

Alternatively, in long-term relationships we go down the path of least resistance. We know that if we do A then B followed by C, he/she will get aroused, have an orgasm and 'that's that'. Sometimes time is limited, especially if we have small children or long days in the office. Tiredness, laziness or a desire for simple effectiveness reduce our sexual repertoire to a small range of predetermined moves. The effect may appear successful – perhaps penetration occurs, perhaps one or the other has an orgasm – but something is missing. What gets left out are spontaneity, improvisation and creativity, and with it the excitement that creates great sex.

So, having examined the problems of pleasure, how can we go about navigating our way back to the type of innocent pursuit of pleasure that we had as children, which was, hopefully, free and self-expressive?

Exercise: Where is Your Pleasure? *(30 minutes)*

In this exercise we invite you to feel your body as you recall past pleasurable experiences, as a stating point to connecting with pleasure in your body in the present. Remember, as with all of this book's exercises, to be gentle with yourself. Not everyone finds such processes easy and some people benefit from doing the exercise several times in order to have a really deep felt sense of their body.

208

1. Take some time to make yourself comfortable. Lie down or sit in a quiet space and close your eyes. You might like to have your notebook and pen close to hand.

2. Begin to connect with your body, noticing your breath as it enters your nostrils. Feel the breath move down into your chest and belly. Bring awareness back to your nose as you exhale, feeling the warm air leaving your nostrils, perhaps feeling it on your upper lip.

3. Become aware of any scent or smell in the room. Notice if you have any tastes on your tongue. Become aware of the sounds around you, however subtle.

4. Notice how your entire body is supported as you are sitting or lying, and the points of contact with the ground. Feel your skin and bring awareness to the sensation of your clothes against it, and how it feels different if the skin is exposed.

5. Become aware of being fully connected with your physical senses.

6. Now cast your mind back to some happy memories of something you enjoyed as a child. Allow images to emerge as vividly as they can. Perhaps you see yourself climbing a tree, eating a lollipop, swimming in the sea, running through long grass or feeling the sand on a beach on your skin.

7. As you do so, notice how your body feels. What sensations do you become aware of? Take your time to feel, so that you know how you experience pleasure in your body.

8. Now move your awareness into your adult life and recall a positive sexual experience. That may be one that you had with a lover or it may be one that you had with yourself. It may even be a sense of your sexual energy even though it might not have looked overtly sexual from the outside. You might want to swap roles as well.

9. Recall the experience and allow images to appear as distinctly as possible. Allow your other senses to be reawakened, too: smell the

memory, taste it. Notice how your body feels now, as you reconnect with that sense-memory. What do you feel in your body and where?

10. Allow yourself to amplify the senses that are awakened. Imagine you are 'turning up the volume' on them. In whatever way feels good for you, intensify the pleasure in your body.

11. If your body wants to move, allow that. If your desire is to make sound, let that come through, too. If you become aroused, that's okay; if you don't, that's okay, too.

12. Feel the response in your body as you recall your experiences as vividly as you can.

13. When you feel ready, without rushing, open your eyes and come back into the space. You might want to take some notes to help you recall what you felt in your body and where you enjoyed the pleasure.

This exercise started with the childhood innocence of pleasure. We hope that it helped you to reconnect with some more pleasure in your body, and to remember what you used to enjoy doing and why it gave you pleasure. Notice that the first experiences of pleasure in childhood are often nonsexual and yet are still felt in the body. When we give ourselves permission to enjoy such innocent pleasures, we open the gateway to other, more adult – yet equally innocent – pleasures such as those in the sensual and sexual realms.

> *The beginning, then, of changing our relationship with pleasure is to broaden our definition of what sexual pleasure is.*

For many, pleasure in sex is strongly linked to genital arousal or the even more limiting idea that it's simply orgasm. Either one is a very limited perspective. Pleasure is a felt sense in the whole body, not just one part and not just the so-called erogenous zones or the genitals.

When we expand our definition of pleasure to include nonsexual sensations, we also enrich our palette of pleasure and allow greater possibility in our physical encounters. Remember, sexual and sensual energies are not the same and pleasure may arise in either place. Just because the feeling changes from sexual to sensual does not mean that it's not pleasure.

Pleasure may also arise in the non-physical, although this is felt in the body as much as physically stimulated pleasures. The pleasure of connection is important for many people. Those feelings of love or intimacy that we all long for, and which may be expressed in both the sexual and in physical closeness, are a potent experience and driver. However, pleasure isn't limited to the physical sense of touch – it applies to all of the senses. For example, to most people a passionate kiss is so pleasurable because it stimulates all five senses – we feel the touch of the tongue and the lips, we taste the other, we smell them, we may hear the sounds of their pleasure, and with our faces close together we see them up close and personal. We find similar parallels in the act of oral sex. This is an act of intimacy that also awakens all the senses. Often it can feel more intimate than penetration (and for many people it is more challenging to enjoy).

What's important to understand about pleasure is that, like sex itself, it has no goal other than the experience itself.

With pleasure there's nowhere to get to, there's no goal. Experiencing pleasure is itself the point of pleasure. Pleasure is less about what's happening and more about our relationship with that experience. If, for example, we perceive pleasure as being related only to orgasm, then we rule out the possibility of pleasure arising in other places. If we feel that only certain situations or emotions may give rise to pleasure, then we limit our capacity to experience it elsewhere.

So, the broader our definition of pleasure, the more pleasure we make available to ourselves.

The more inclusive our umbrella of pleasure can become, the more we can enjoy life itself. This takes us back to the enthusiasm for life and the natural curiosity we felt as children.

Exercise: Body Mapping (45 minutes)

This exercise makes a great kick-starter for having new experiences of pleasure away from the direct erogenous zones and for feeling pleasure in different ways throughout your body. You may be surprised to find that areas of your body you had previously ignored can become new sources of pleasure. Sometimes the pleasure may be sensual, at other times it may feel sexual. Either way, this exercise can be a powerful means to reactivate your pleasure and enhance it.

The exercise is done most effectively with a partner, but you can also do it on your own.

1. Make sure you have some quiet, private time and prepare your space by creating a sensual atmosphere – light some candles, turn on some sensual music, perhaps light some aromatic oils and so on.

2. If you're working with a partner, decide which one of you will 'give' first and which will 'receive'. The receiver will lie down however they feel comfortable, in whatever state of undress feels right for them.

3. As giver, your purpose is to offer your partner varying types of touch on different parts of their body.

4. As receiver, your job is to offer feedback about the touch your partner gives you. You'll do this by scoring on a scale of +3 to –3. If the touch feels neutral in terms pleasure, you'll give a score of 0. If that particular type of touch is slightly enjoyable, you'll give +1, if it's very enjoyable this will become +2 and if intensely pleasurable it will be +3. Similarly, for touch that you find unpleasant, you'll reply using the negative scale of –1 through to –3, which is something akin to 'Stop that right now!' If you want to make the score more accurate, you can also halve numbers or give fractions.

5. As giver, use your imagination to try out different ways of touching: you can stroke, rub, tease, pinch, caress, nibble, or blow warm or cold air with your mouth. You don't have to limit yourself to using your own body to touch. You may like to try using different materials such as feathers, silk, cold metal or something warm. You could take a sip of a warm drink into your mouth: after letting it warm your mouth you'll give a different type of mouth-to-skin contact than usual. Similarly, ice cubes can feel very stimulating.

6. Avoid the obvious areas of the body that you might first be drawn to, such as the genitals or breasts. Areas that are hidden away, such as the back of the knees or the armpits, can offer surprisingly pleasurable zones for touch.

7. Both partners: give yourself permission to be playful! There's no way to get this exercise wrong. Simply go with what you feel like doing and enjoy the exploration.

8. When the exercise feels complete for you, thank your generous partner, and take some time to debrief the experience and share what you learned about yourself. You might want to swap roles as well.

Some touches may feel unpleasant – but even this will help you to learn about what your body enjoys and what it doesn't. Try not to see an unpleasant type of touch as something negative. It's simply information – now you know for next time.

Although the exercise is focused on the sensation of touch, you can also perform something similar with smells or with taste. If you have a partner and want to try smell or taste, it can be great fun to blindfold them (with their consent) and feed them things that they don't know in advance (having checked for any allergies). When we're blindfolded, we can't rely on sight so this tends to awaken the other senses and enhance our awareness of their capacity for pleasure.

It's important that we have a conscious relationship with our ability to experience pleasure, so before doing the exercise, consider whether you're open to pleasure arising in new ways or you're attached to the safety of having pleasure in the same ways that you always have. Can you allow yourself to be curious about your pleasure or do you feel the need to limit it? If you find yourself in the latter category, you might want to re-examine your relationship with pleasure, based on the ideas earlier in this chapter, to see how it became limited in the first place. Can you allow yourself to reconnect with that innocent, childlike exploration of pleasure?

ORGASM – OR NOT...

So what about orgasm? Orgasm is perceived by most people to be a goal – somewhere to get to. As we've mentioned, this can easily become a performance issue, either for oneself or with the idea of 'giving' someone else an orgasm. But this is a misconception, again popular in media and pornography.

You can't give someone else an orgasm. It's their orgasm.
How can you give them something that is already theirs?

Orgasm is simply an experience of pleasure – one of many pleasures we might enjoy during a sexual experience. Orgasm is not a necessity for having great sex. It's something we allow to arise within us – or not. Yes, a partner can create a safe space that allows the other's natural orgasmic response to arise, but a person's orgasm is much more about their own relationship with their pleasure than another person's skills in the bedroom.

There are many blocks to orgasm and they could form the subject of an entire book by themselves. We've already discussed how fear of being shamed for expressing our sexuality or fear of loss of control can shut down our aliveness, including our orgasmic response. Orgasm is a letting go, a loss of the ego's control and ultimately of non-being, the greatest fear that a person can have. This is why in French it's referred to as *la petite mort* – 'the little death'. When we let go into orgasmic bliss, we surrender to the not-yet-known, a sensing of something beyond oneself and a gateway into the vastness of the universe. It is, in effect, an out-of-body experience. The word ecstatic, often used to describe orgasmic states, means most literally to stand beside oneself. Such profound experiences can feel terrifying as well as deeply pleasurable.

Once more we find that the impulse for pleasure is, in its highest form, a call to connect with our existential longings, our deepest yearnings, a desire for connection with self and the experience of losing oneself in something greater.

In 'real sex', which is felt and expressed authentically moment to moment, we encourage you to drop the idea of orgasm as the focus or even 'the point' of sex. This approach removes a lot of the pressure of orgasm-related performance, and encourages each person to take full responsibility for their own pleasure and not expect someone else to do it to them.

Exercise: Orgasm-Free Sex *(Ongoing for a month)*

For the final exercise in this book we invite you to suspend altogether your desire for an orgasm and see what else can emerge when you stop pursuing it.

Whether you are in a partnership or alone, we recommend you try for at least 30 days to have sexual experiences without orgasm becoming involved.

I. Allow yourself to self-pleasure or to engage in whatever sexual expression feels good for you but does not in any way focus on orgasm, either in yourself or your partner.

2. Make sure that you follow your pleasure. Allow your body to move, and slowly and gently feel into the pleasure that your body can give you, but don't in any way become goal-oriented.

3. Avoid going into the performance of trying to please your partner. Keep your focus on your own pleasure and be present with yourself in that. The more you are present with yourself, the more you can be present with another person. The more you focus on your own pleasure, the more authentically you can express yourself in intimacy.

4. If you notice an impulse to move towards orgasm, see if you can stay in the moment. It's not wrong if an orgasm comes naturally, but don't make any effort to have one.

5. We recommend that you keep an ongoing reflection in your notebook about what happens in you during this exercise, and between you and your partner if you are sharing the exercise with someone.

It can really make a difference to try this exercise repeatedly.

The more you can move away from the goal of orgasm in sex, the more subtle and pleasurable sensations you will become aware of.

When we focus on orgasm, we limit the range of our possible experiences of pleasure to those related to orgasm. When we let go of this focus on a narrow band of awareness, we allow something else to emerge. We can begin to feel more subtle and delicate sensations in our body. We can make space so that other experiences of sensation and connection, with both ourselves and with our partner, can come to the forefront of our awareness. We let go of the idea of needing to 'get somewhere' in sex and this creates a more expansive experience of pleasure in the whole body, and of a deeper sense of relaxation and connection. It broadens the possibility of sexual pleasure into a richer and more varied palette.

This chapter is aimed to help you to broaden your experience and definition of what pleasure can be. In the exercises, we've linked pleasure not only to sexual experience, but also to other bodily pleasures as well.

> ***Similarly, the point of sex is not having sex, and it certainly isn't orgasm.***

Ultimately, pleasure – similar to our definition of desire – is about coming into connection with oneself. When we're in connection with ourselves, especially with our body, we have the capacity to feel pleasure.

> ***Pleasure is a flow of energy; it is not fixed.***

What feels good today may not feel as enjoyable tomorrow, with another person or in a different setting. Pleasure, like desire, is fluid. The more we can open up to a greater range of what might constitute pleasure, the more we give ourselves permission to enjoy it. The potential for pleasure arises in every moment, no matter where we are or what we're doing. Pleasure is always a possibility.

The more we can slow ourselves down and listen to our body, the more we can allow the pleasure impulse to arise in us, the more fluid we can allow its expression to be, the more pleasure we can permit ourselves to have. Instead of focusing on where we think pleasure should go, stay with the feeling of where pleasure is in the moment. In this way we stay present with ourselves and this gives us the ability to be present with our partner, too. Pleasure and presence are closely linked. We cannot be truly in our pleasure if we're not present in our body in each moment.

What matters when it comes to pleasure is our ability to suspend judgment, to simply listen to our body's impulses and follow them.

This is the art of pleasure. The art of sex is pleasure, too. It's not about technique and it's not about performing. In a way, it's as simple as allowing our body's natural passions and aliveness to be fully expressed.

Epilogue

EROS RESTORED

This book is inherently about Eros. It's about this powerful force that runs through our minds, emotions and bodies, that defines our deepest being and makes us want to be alive.

> *Eros energy is our life-force energy.*
> *It's the energy of expression, creation,*
> *expansion, connection and growth.*

When we're in the flow of our aliveness, it's this energy that gives us aliveness and a sense of meaning, belonging and engagement in our life. It makes us want to get out of bed in the morning and, playfully, back into it later in the day.

However, we've learned that Eros has, effectively, to be suppressed, for a number of complex historical and sociological reasons, some of which we've described in this book. We've shown how pornography and the media present a distorted version of sexuality as something that has to exist in the shadowlands, as something we just don't talk about. And we've shown how this societal fear of sexuality and self-expression has been passed on to us from our parents, who learned it from their parents and so on – dating a long way back in Western culture.

Sexuality has been taken hostage in a
battle of religion and social power and is
still so, exploited by commercialism while
being kept under strict societal control.

Even now, well into the 21st century with all its technological, scientific and philosophical achievements, we're not free, erotic, natural sexual beings. We're carrying shame, taboo and fears around our sexuality that prevent us from fully owning it. We hide it, we don't talk about it, we act it out in the shadows and in the awkward privacy of our bedrooms, thinking we're the only one having a problem with sexuality or feeling confused and insecure. We suffer under the illusion that everyone else is having great sex, and that we should live up to the idealized and distorted imagery presented by the media or in pornography. We have so wholly accepted society's need to censor our sexuality that we have internalized that censorship to the point where we often see clients in our practice who struggle to stand up and say the simple words: 'I am a sexual woman' or 'I am a sexual man.'

It's no surprise, then, that sex is such a battlefield, because whoever 'owns' our Eros owns our power.

When we fully own our Eros, our life-
force energy, we cannot be controlled.

When we fully own our own Eros, we'll have a clear sense of direction in life. We'll know what we want and what we don't want and we'll be able to communicate it and hold clear in our boundaries in doing so. We'll know our value, because we can show up in the world without shame, without needing to hide parts of ourselves. We'll feel connected to ourselves and sensitive to others in a way that makes us profoundly empowered.

This is why, as sexual psychotherapists on a mission, we wrote this book. We are passionate about social change. We are passionate about restoring Eros and taking back that power for each and every individual as the birthright it is. We are passionate about helping people to experience the joy of freedom in sexual expression because it sets us all free at a very deep level.

Remember the image of the temple that we presented in this book's introduction – the base being the foundations of the cultural values we stand on, the pillars the different ways we're reaching for what is at the top of the temple, the pediment our deepest longing for meaning, love and connection, our sacred relationship with life? As it stands right now, the pillar of our sexuality is broken. It's not fully accessible and accepted as a way for us to reach for what we really want. Sexuality and desire remain 'edgy', no matter how natural we try to be around them. Just notice for a moment the endless ways in which you edit or contemplate editing yourself in a simple thing such as reading this book. Would you be able to leave it lying on the coffee table or to read it on the train? Or are there no issues for you in wanting to gain knowledge about sex? Our guess is that only a very few readers will be completely free of their own internal judgment. This is why the pillar of sexuality is so essential: it is where we'll find our greatest inhibitions.

No other topic is as contentious as sex. Yet no other topic has the capacity to empower us, and to offer us such an effective and rapid tool for personal growth and development.

Yet you made a choice: you bought this book and read it. The calling for freedom in self-expression was stronger than your desire to edit yourself. We hope this book speaks to some of your deepest longings, to yearnings of which you were perhaps unaware at a conscious level before you read it. Our guess is that, somewhere within, you've realized that until sex and intimacy unfold their full potential within you, something will be missing in your life. We believe and know from our professional experience that it's in the shadows of our unconscious mind that we find our greatest potential. It's when we fully embrace all that we are that we become all that we can be.

It is our sincere hope that this book has helped you to reconnect more deeply with yourself, and inspired and supported you in reclaiming your identity as a fully erotic, sexual being. We hope that the exercises took you deeper into yourself, that reading the book became a felt, embodied experience and that you met parts of yourself you might have known were lurking in the shadows but which have now been able to shine with the full potential of their innate core qualities.

An essential message of this book that runs as an undercurrent through all of its chapters is that we need to come out of the mind that is constantly assessing, judging and comparing our experience and into an embodied presence with yourself and your partner – to be in the flow of Eros, not simply to think, allow or perform sex.

This is our final invitation to you: to reflect on what has changed. What have you learned about your desires? What are your golden and shadow motivations for having sex? Have you been able to acknowledge your 'shadow motivations' and thus transform them into real potential for growth? Did you realize why you are having sex and what it is that you really want? And, most importantly: how has that insight manifested in your erotic life?

Equally, we would ask: what did you learn about your sexual self? What 'mini-characters' did you discover? Which ones are you comfortable with expressing and which are yet to be embodied? What parts of yourself did you uncover – perhaps unexpressed but waiting to be met? When you stop editing yourself, what are your sexual fantasies and can you now allow them to be expressed a little more than before?

Have you developed a self-pleasuring practice and a sexual relationship with yourself? Are you still waiting for someone else to make you feel sexual, or do you own the Eros energy in you already? What steps could you take to begin to reclaim your Eros energy for yourself rather than waiting for someone else to awaken it within you?

How is your relationship with your body? Do you love yourself and the stories of your life that your body is holding? Are you able to be turned on by yourself? Can you find beauty in your body and love it, no matter how it looks? Is your body an external image to you, a vehicle for your mind, or do you fully inhabit it and allow the pleasures it has to offer? Are you treating yourself as your own first lover, caring and caressing yourself into loving presence?

How much are you able to be present, with yourself or another? Do you leave your body in sex, losing your presence to mental images or anxieties about performance? How effective did you find the embodiment exercises, where we invited you to connect with your body? What about when we suggested you practise erotic mindfulness and notice the Eros energy in your body? Did these exercises teach you to feel what is going on in your body instead of running away from it? Are you able to hold both the uncomfortable feelings and sensations of pleasure? Do you stay connected to yourself and present with your lover in a new way?

Have you exercised staying authentic by clearly expressing your desires and boundaries? Are you beginning to catch yourself when denying, pleasing and pretending, or when keeping silent even though something needs to be spoken? Do you take responsibility for your sexual identity or do you sit around and wait for others to do so?

Is shame still in charge of your sexuality or can you give yourself permission to be the fully sexual being that you are? Have you become aware of the judgmental inner voices that stop you from freely expressing your desires, and have you worked out who put them there in the first place? Has that awareness allowed you to make different choices, to have different experiences?

And has that led to greater pleasure? Have you discovered something new about yourself by contemplating the relationship you have with pleasure? Do you believe you deserve it? Do you ultimately believe you have a right to exist, in your body, on this planet, and to enjoy it – or does life have to be a little hard for you to feel safe? If so, what have you done to change that belief?

We hope that most of these questions will now be easier for you to answer. Maybe you're not entirely able to give yourself the answers that you'd like but can at least agree that you have an awareness that something has changed and that other bits are on the move. Personal development does not usually happen overnight. Remember to be gentle with yourself. In order for growth to show up as real changes in your life, it has to happen organically.

One of our golden rules in therapy is
that awareness creates conscious choice,
and choice leads to empowerment.

This means that in each and every moment, you have the possibility of making a different, conscious choice instead of following the usual patterns of unconscious beliefs.

This book is about helping you to understand how those beliefs prevent you from being the empowered human being you can be and from being every bit the sexual person that you are. If the book has been successful, it will have helped you to see how you inhibit yourself from allowing Eros into your life and it will have given you a range of tools and ideas that can allow you to fulfil your potential to engage with life and with your Eros energy. We hope you've reconnected with your deepest longings and been given the means to continue your journey towards reaching them.

The reward for reconnecting and allowing that deep yearning is the capacity to re-establish your relationship with your sexuality as one of the pillars of your sacred relationship with life. From this place you will be empowered to experience yourself in ways that might previously have seemed impossible. What you can achieve when you connect with your sexual self in its fullness is beyond the realm of the sexual. When we're in our sexual power we're also in our personal power, the power of choice for our actions, the power to create our life experience and the power to choose loving, intimate relationships.

By using our Seven Keys to 'real sex' you will be able to connect with your personal and sexual powers at a level higher than anything you previously imagined possible. The more you allow space for being exactly who you are, the more you inspire this in your lovers and your loved ones and the more this will come back to you in love, depth and richness of connection. We wish you joy and gentleness on your journey into your fully empowered sexual self.

References

1. Gardner, H., 1993. *Frames of Mind: Theory of Multiple Intelligences.* London: Fontana Press.

2. Cozolino, L., 2010. *The Neuroscience of Psychotherapy: Healing the Social Brain.* 2nd revised edition. NY: W.W. Norton & Company.

3. Creswell *et al*, 2013. Experimental manipulation of primary sexual reward buffers cortisol responses to psychosocial stress in men. *Psychosomatic Medicine*, 75, 397–403.

4. The National Survey of Sexual Attitudes and Lifestyles (Natsal III, 2010–2012).

5. Royal College of Obstetricians and Gynaecologists, 2013. *Ethical considerations in relation to female genital cosmetic surgery (FGCS).* [pdf] Available at:<http://tinyurl.com/l28apnm> [Accessed 20 March 2017].

6. Hayes *et al*, 2006. Original Research–Epidemiology: What Can Prevalence Studies Tell Us About Female Sexual Difficulty and Dysfunction? *Journal of Sexual Medicine* (3), 589–595.

7. Kratochvíl S., 1994. Orgasmic Expulsions in Women. *Ceskoslovenaká psychiatrie* 90 (2), 71–77.

8. Voon *et al*, 2014. Neural correlates of sexual cue reactivity in individuals with and without compulsive sexual behaviours. *PLOS One* [e-journal] 9 (7). Available at: <http://tinyurl.com/m5fono5> [Accessed 20 March 2017].

9. Haworth, A., *The Guardian* (20 October 2013) *Why have young people in Japan stopped having sex?* [online]. Available at: < http://tinyurl.com/zps34ch> [Accessed 20 March 2017].

10. Successful Motivation International, Inc., *Wheel of Life*® [online] Available at: < http://www.lmi-world.com/smi-wheel-of-life/> [Accessed 20 March 2017].

11. Siegel, D.J., 2013. *The Mindful Therapist: A Clinician's Guide to Mindsight and Neural Integration.* NY: W.W. Norton & Company.

12. Kinsey, A.C., Pomeroy, W.B. and Martin, C.E., 1948. *Sexual Behavior in the Human Male.* Philadelphia: W.B. Saunders Company.

13. Kinsey, A.C., Pomeroy, W.B. and Martin, C.E., 1953. *Sexual Behavior in the Human Female.* Philadelphia: W.B. Saunders Company.

14. Hite, S., 1976. *The Hite Report on Female Sexuality.* London: Macmillan.

15. Hite, S., 1981. *The Hite Report on Male Sexuality.* New York: Alfred A. Knopf.

ABOUT THE AUTHORS

Irina Smirnova

Mike Lousada was born in Somerset, UK, and brought up in a middle-class household where sex was viewed, at least, with suspicion if not contempt. The resulting body and sexual shame took many years to heal, but having transformed himself through a combination of psychotherapy and other healing modalities, he is now passionate about supporting this transformation in others.

Mike has trained as a psychotherapist, clinical sexologist and bodyworker, and has developed a cutting-edge modality, Psychosexual Somatics®, to support this growth in himself and others. *Psychologies* magazine described Mike as 'one of the most respected sex therapists in the world'. He currently lives in London with his wife and co-author, Louise Mazanti.

Louise Mazanti PhD was born into a Danish/Catalan family, and grew up in Denmark. Having achieved an international academic career, at the age of 35 she had a spiritual awakening that called her to question the many things she had compromised to gain her academic reputation – her identity as a woman, her relationship with her body, her sexuality and her spirituality. Louise subsequently retrained as a transpersonal psychotherapist, in esoteric philosophy and energy psychology. Her relationship with Mike, and their deepening in love and intimacy, has created a powerful tool for personal and spiritual growth.

Mike and Louise's relationship forms the ground from which their work arises, learning together to heal themselves and others through intimacy. Together they teach around the world, including at the Esalen Institute in California.

www.mazantilousada.com

HAY HOUSE

Look within

Join the conversation about latest products,
events, exclusive offers and more.

f   Hay House UK

   @HayHouseUK

   @hayhouseuk

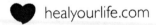   healyourlife.com

We'd love to hear from you!

CPSIA information can be obtained
at www.ICGtesting.com
Printed in the USA
FSOW01n0736260617
35574FS